GETTING STARTED WITH Coding

Camille McCue, PhD

WILEY

GETTING STARTED WITH CODING

Published by
John Wiley & Sons, Inc.
111 River Street
Hoboken, NJ 07030-5774

www.wiley.com

Library of Congress Control Number: 201594739

ISBN 9781119177173 (pbk); 9781119177194 (epdf); 9781119177203 (epub)

This book was produced using the Myriad Pro typeface for the body text and callouts, and Bangers for the chapter titles and subheads.

Manufactured in the United States of America

10 9 8 7 6 5 4 3 2 1

CONTENTS

INTRODUCTION

SO YOU WANT TO GET STARTED WITH CODING! Writing computer programs, or *coding*, is a skill that will take you from a user of technology to a maker of technology. Coding is a skill that is fun, creative, and productive. By discovering the language of the computer, you become capable of inventing toys, games, and apps that you can share with, well … everyone!

ABOUT THIS BOOK

There are so many computer languages you can use to get started with coding. What you'll find in this book is an introductory treatment of coding in a single programming language — a teaching language, called MicroWorlds EX, that is conceptually transferrable to every other programming language. It's *easy to learn* because the vocabulary and punctuation look like regular words and symbols. And it's fun to do because you can add graphics, motion, and sound to make your projects into real apps.

Getting Started with Coding is put together as a series of projects with steps for constructing each project from start to finish. Projects are crafted to make sure you learn key ideas you'll need over and over again when coding. Every project begins with a game plan you can follow to stay organized as you work. And every game plan features *coding* and graphics activities to complete. Best of all, projects can be customized to bring to life the craziest ideas your imagination can concoct!

Here's what you need to do the projects in this book:

- A computer running a reasonably modern version of a Windows or Mac OS X operating system
- MicroWorlds EX software (free with this book!)

» An Internet connection to download the MicroWorlds EX software

As you work through each project, keep in mind the following writing conventions:

Code and web addresses are in `monofont`. If you're reading this as an ebook, you can click web addresses, like www.dummies.com, to visit that website.

Some figures will have a magnifying glass, like you see here. The glass is drawing attention to the parts of the screen that you use. The highlighted text draws your attention to the figure.

I also give you instructions like "Drag a Y into the X" or "Click the X category and then click X." Or I may simply tell you to click a link or a tab.

Finally, every project wraps up with a last look at the project's big ideas in coding. The big ideas consist of both codes and concepts you'll find useful for future projects.

ABOUT YOU

Everybody has to start somewhere, right? I had to start writing this book by assuming that you can do this stuff:

» Type on a computer and use a mouse. Your experience can be either on a Windows or Mac system — either one will do! Instructions for coding each project are written for both platforms, and figures are shown for MicroWorlds EX operating on a Mac.

- You're capable of installing software, because you will be installing the MicroWorlds EX program on your computer.

Further, I've made some assumptions with regard to your entering into the world of coding:

- You've played games on a computer, so you know how people interact with computer games (which is different than how people play video games using a gaming console).
- You're comfortable with basic math, math operations such as adding whole numbers, and logical operations such as comparing two whole numbers. I introduce algebraic variables in this book, but you don't need to have any prior knowledge of variables.

Lastly, if you struggle with spelling, you may need to spend extra time troubleshooting your code for misspellings. A programming language doesn't understand spelling errors, but it can give you clues about which commands it doesn't understand.

ABOUT THE ICONS

As you read through the projects in this book, you'll see a few icons. The icons point out different things:

Watch out! This icon marks important information that you can use to avoid common pitfalls when coding.

The Remember icon marks concepts you've encountered before and should keep in mind while coding.

The Tip icon marks advice and shortcuts that will help you create code and graphics quickly and easily.

The Fun with Code icon describes how the coding you're doing relates to the bigger picture of computer programming.

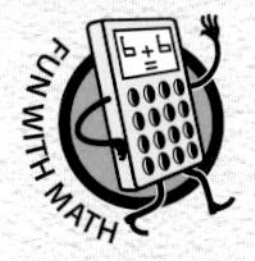

The Fun with Math icon describes the everyday math you use while coding computer programs. Finally, you see how that stuff really is used!

THE FIRST STEP

After you gain a little experience coding, there are a bazillion new directions you can go, from learning more advanced concepts in MicroWorlds EX to tackling more challenging programming languages. I congratulate you on taking the first step!

PROJECT 1 GET STARTED

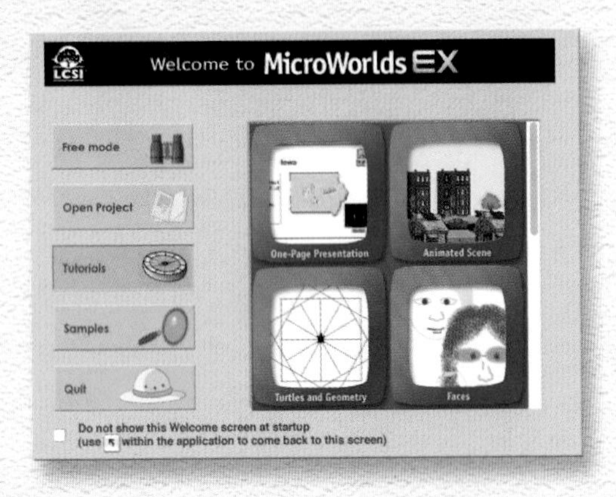

IT USED TO BE ENOUGH TO READ, WRITE, AND DO MATHEMATICS TO BE EDUCATED. Those three skills were the tools we needed to communicate with other human beings in our world. But now, the world is full of intelligent beings that aren't human — they are computers. Computers don't think for themselves just *yet*, but they communicate with each other and with us through *computer programming languages*. Learning to communicate with technology takes a new skill called *coding*, so that you can speak the language of computers.

In this chapter, I tell you what coding is and tell you the types of projects you can make. Then, I show you MicroWorlds EX, which is the software that you will use to create the projects in this book.

UNDERSTANDING WHAT CODING IS

Coding means writing instructions for a piece of technology — usually a computer. The computer uses the instructions to perform a task. A computer programming language provides the *vocabulary* (words) and *syntax* (rules and punctuation) for communicating with a computer. The instructions that you create and that the computer reads are a *computer program*.

LEARNING TO CODE WITH MICROWORLDS EX

To get started coding, you need only a computer, the programming language software, and an up-to-date version of a Windows or Mac OS X operating system. Some languages, such as Scratch, operate in a web browser, so you must also have a browser such as Firefox to work with those options.

The programming language software that you will use with this book is MicroWorlds EX. Once you have installed MicroWorlds EX, you don't need a login and you don't need web access.

EXAMINING WHY MICROWORLDS EX IS A GOOD LANGUAGE TO START WITH

MicroWorlds EX is a teaching language that has been used with new coders for a long time. It is a perfect first language for many reasons:

- It uses everyday words and abbreviations for *commands*.
- It isn't picky about capitalization.
- It keeps punctuation simple.
- It has drag-and-drop palettes and also areas for writing lines of code.
- It has built-in paint tools and a Shape Editor for painting backgrounds and characters.
- It can import sounds or you can record your own. It also has a text-to-speech command.
- It has built-in error checking and troubleshooting help.

TAKING A LOOK AT WHAT PROJECTS YOU CAN MAKE

By working in MicroWorlds EX, you'll discover important programming ideas that allow you to make cool projects *now*. These ideas also set the stage for more advanced coding in the future.

What kinds of things can you make? Everything! Up until now, you've probably been a user or consumer of technology. You play games, communicate with friends via social media, and order goods online. But by learning to code, you are now a *maker* of software, a producer in the world of technology!

In this book, you will make three different types of projects:

- *Toys* are things you play with. They have no specific goal or scoring: Quick Draw (Project 2), Ha Ha Headlines (Project 5), and Hungry Bobo (Project 7) are all toys.
- *Games* have a goal and sometimes a score or a beat-the-clock challenge. Games offer challenges that can be won or lost. Space Race (Project 4) and Find Friendly (Project 6) are both games.
- *Simulations* (sims) are programs that are meant to model the real world. Coin Flipper (Project 3) is a simulation.

Ultimately, the coding skills you learn in this book are just the beginning. I hope you create all sorts of new programs that are wilder and wackier than anything contained in these pages. And I hope you level up and tackle learning new programming languages as you increase your skill level in the coming years.

GETTING STARTED WITH MICROWORLDS EX

Your purchase of this book comes with a 35-day, 90-saves-allowed trial of MicroWorlds EX, so you can work through all the projects at the rate of approximately one project every five or six days. At any time, you can purchase MicroWorlds EX at a deep discount so you can continue developing your coding skills creating new projects to share with friends and family.

DOWNLOADING AND INSTALLING THE SOFTWARE

To download and install the trial version of MicroWorlds EX, navigate to www.dummies.com/go/gettingstartedwithcoding. Then follow the onscreen download and installation instructions.

For PCs, MicroWorlds EX is supported on Windows 7, Windows 8, and Windows 8.1. For Macs, MicroWorlds EX is supported on OS X Version 10.7 and later.

STARTING A PROJECT

After you've installed it, follow these steps to start MicroWorlds EX:

1 Click the yellow backpack icon (shown in the margin).

The backpack serves as the icon for MicroWorlds EX because objects in this programming language are called turtles, and every turtle totes a backpack carrying important information just like your backpack.

As MicroWorlds EX starts, you see the blue MicroWorlds EX splash screen.

2 Click the splash screen to dismiss it.

A yellow Welcome to MicroWorlds EX screen opens and presents several options to you.

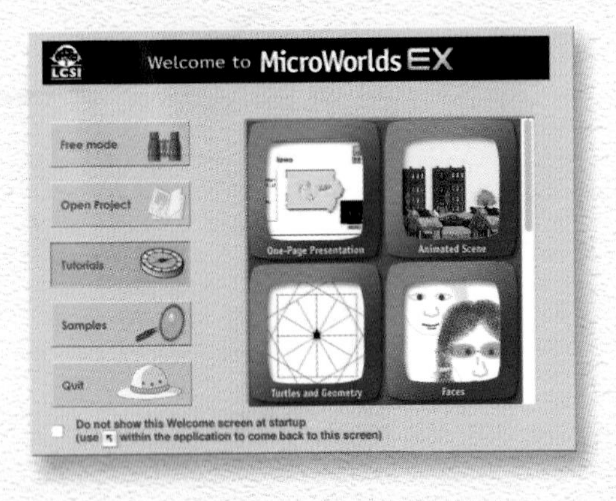

3 Choose Free Mode to start a new project, or Open Project to open a saved project.

Once you choose an option, you see the MicroWorlds EX interface. Free Mode presents an empty interface because you haven't created any code or graphics yet.

GETTING TO KNOW THE INTERFACE

Note the following key areas of the MicroWorlds EX interface:

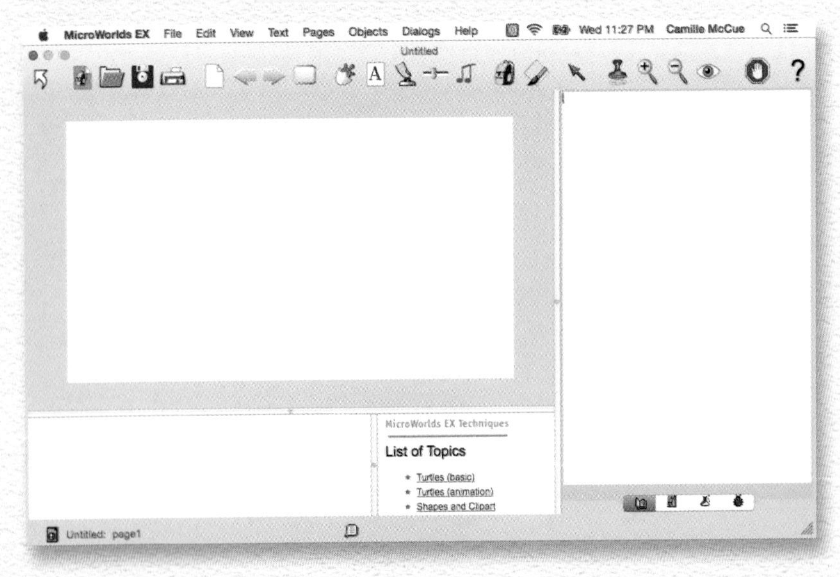

- **Menu bar:** Contains menus for opening and saving files, editing (copying and pasting), changing the view of the interface, formatting text, creating and naming new pages, creating new objects and dialogs, and help.
- **Toolbar:** Contains button versions of File items on the menu bar. A few buttons merit special mention:
  - *Regular pointer:* Sometimes the mouse pointer is a regular (arrow) pointer for dragging a turtle or button to a new position. Other times, it appears as a cursor in places where you can type. And sometimes, it is a hand for placing shapes in the workspace. Press the Regular Pointer button to get the Regular Pointer back.
  - *Eye Tool:* Click the Eye Tool button and then click an element in the workspace to change information about it. This button is also useful for locating hidden objects (turtles) — just click the Eye Tool to reveal their locations.
  - *Stop All:* This button stops program execution. When characters are flying around the screen, click Stop All to halt everything.
  - *Presentation Mode:* Use this button to view your project as an end user would see it. Press the Escape key (Esc) to return to the regular MicroWorlds EX view.
- **Project title and page number:** The project title appears at the top of the MicroWorlds EX interface and in the lower-left corner. This second location, called the status bar, also shows the page number of the current page within the project; for example, page1.
- **Workspace:** This is where you create the physical appearance of your project. Here, you can add a background and then create turtles, buttons, and other objects. At the start of a new project, you can change the size of the workspace.

- **Command Center:** This region is used for several different purposes:
  - You can try out a command or snippet of code and instantly see the results.
  - You can issue a command that doesn't need to be reused. For example, if you've created ten asteroids and you want all of them to fly in the same direction, you can command everyone to head in a specific direction and be done with it.
  - You can see any error messages. If MicroWorlds EX finds a problem with your code, it will tell you in the Command Center.
- **Panes:** The right side of the MicroWorlds EX interface features four panes stacked on top of each other. Only one pane shows at a time, and you can move among panes by clicking these tabs at the bottom-right side of the interface:
  - *Procedures:* For writing new commands
  - *Project:* For viewing all pages and elements in a project
  - *Processes:* For viewing program processes as they execute
  - *Shapes:* For creating shapes for objects and editing shapes
- Detailed use of each pane will be discussed further in the projects.

The divider bars between the workspace, Command Center, and panes can be moved to change your view of each area as needed.

GETTING HELP

This book covers just a few key MicroWorlds EX commands. The Help menu at the MicroWorlds EX menu bar contains an option for viewing the entire language vocabulary, sorted alphabetically. Each MicroWorlds EX command is explained and shows and example. I am constantly using this resource to find new MicroWorlds EX commands (*primitives*) I need in my code. I hope you find it as useful as I do! The Help menu also offers help in fundamentals, programming, and more techniques.

Another great help resource for learning how to use primitives is available as you code: With your cursor in the Command Center or project Procedures pane, hover over any MicroWorlds EX primitive — a tool tip appears with information telling you how to format the primitive.

Additionally, the startup screen of MicroWorlds EX gives you access to useful tutorials and samples. Every example you can view and play with is a learning opportunity. I also encourage you to modify the code of each example to develop your coding skills.

Lastly, the MicroWorlds EX website located at www.microworlds.com is a great source of links to examples from kid coders around the world — take a look for new ideas!

COMING UP WITH YOUR IDEAS AND YOUR PROJECTS

As you get started with the projects in this book, keep in mind that you can add your own creativity. Lots of apps have the same code, but feature different characters, backgrounds, and stories. I encourage you to make every project your own.

Now get coding!

PROJECT 2 QUICK DRAW

DO YOU LIKE TO DRAW AND PAINT? Let's make a drawing tool for making cool computer art! You'll code an app for a user to create digital art with colorful lines and shapes. This project will also introduce you to fun coding concepts you will use in all your programming work. Let's go!

BRAINSTORM

Follow the steps here, but feel free to make changes! Try new colors and different turn angles. Add buttons. This is your project. Be creative!

GAME PLAN

For each project, we'll share a game plan for building the app. The game plan shows coding (computer programming) and graphics (backgrounds, characters, and buttons) needed to make the app. This is not a flow chart of how the app operates. It is a work plan you can follow to stay organized.

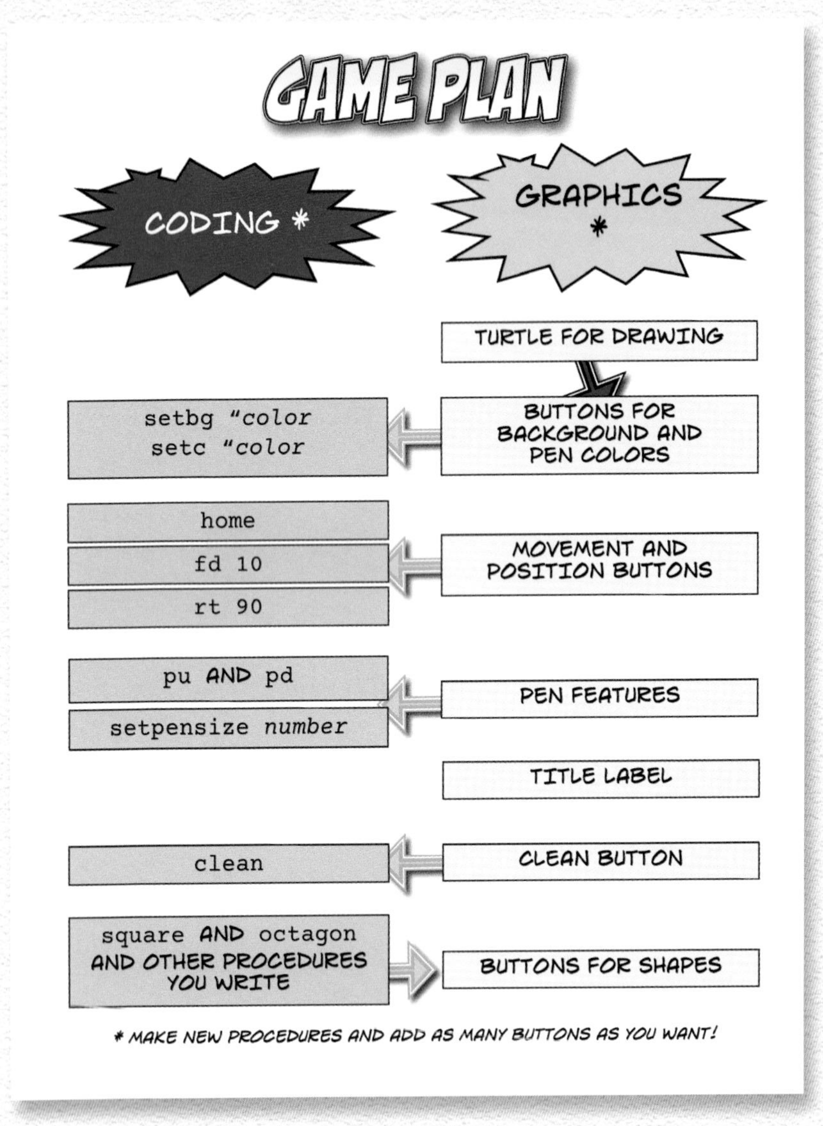

START A NEW PROJECT

Begin your Quick Draw app by starting a new project:

1. **Start MicroWorlds EX.**
2. **On the yellow MicroWorlds EX startup screen, select Free Mode.**

   A new project opens.
3. **From the menu bar, choose File and then choose New Project Size.**
4. **Pick any screen size you want!**

The big, white area that appears is the *workspace*.

Project size can only be set at the start of a new project.

ADD A TURTLE

Programming languages have ways to make objects you can move around in the workspace. In MicroWorlds EX, an object is called a *turtle.*

Create a turtle object for your Quick Draw:

1. **On the toolbar, click the Create a Turtle button.**
2. **Click in the workspace. A turtle appears.**
3. **Drag the turtle anywhere in the workspace.**
4. **Click and drag the turtle's nose around in a circle to point it in any direction.**

CODE IN THE COMMAND CENTER

In MicroWorlds EX, coding and other communication is done in the Command Center just below the workspace. While coding, you'll work with two types of commands:

» **Primitives:** Built-in commands.

» **Procedures:** New commands you create.

When you type a command into the Command Center and then press Enter (if you're on a Windows computer) or Return (if you're on a Mac computer), the command will *execute,* or run.

SET BACKGROUND COLOR

When drawing and painting, you want a nice canvas! Type the *set background* command (`setbg`) at the Command Center to color the workspace:

```
setbg "yellow
```

Try other colors like `green`, `red`, `orange`, `lime`, and `violet`.

In the Command Center, you can type a new line of code each time or just type changes in a command you already made, and then press Enter (Windows) or Return (Mac) to run it.

Computer programming languages have *syntax* — the rules for "speaking" the language. The parts of syntax are

- **Grammar:** Where the words go.
- **Punctuation:** Where to put parentheses, brackets, commas, and quotes.

Programming languages check your code for errors. If you get an error message, you must fix, or debug, your code to make it run. In MicroWorlds EX, error messages appear in the Command Center — read them to see what changes you need to make.

CHANGE PEN COLOR

Painters need different colors in their palettes to paint with! Type a *set color* command (`setc`) at the Command Center to change the color of the turtle and its pen:

```
setc "red
```

Try other colors, like `blue` or `magenta`. The color of the turtle is the same as the color of its painting pen.

SEND AN OBJECT HOME

Move the turtle to the center of the workspace and point it up by typing the command `home` at the Command Center.

DRAW LINES

Make the turtle walk in lines by typing a forward (`fd`) or backward (`bk`) command and corresponding value at the Command Center:

- `fd 10` means move forward 10 steps.
- `bk 10` means move backward 10 steps.

The maximum value for forward and backward is 9999.

The MicroWorlds EX workspace is like a flat map of Earth. If a turtle walks off one side of the workspace, it comes back on the opposite side.

TURN

Turn the turtle using these *turn* commands at the Command Center:

- `rt` *or* `lt`: `rt 90` *or* `lt 90`

  These commands turn the turtle right or left. They translate to *turn right 90 degrees* or *turn left 90 degrees*. Try other degree angles, such as `45`, `180`, `270`, and `360`. Turtle turns are from the viewpoint of the turtle.

Angles are measured in units called degrees. *There are 360 degrees in a circle. To make a turtle face the opposite direction, give the command* `rt 180` *or* `lt 180`.

CHANGE PEN FEATURES

Make the turtle use its pen by typing a *pen* command at the Command Center:

» `pd` *or* `pu`

These commands mean *pen up* and *pen down*. Put the pen down and then walk the turtle forward or backward to see the turtle draw as it moves.

» `setpensize`: `setpensize 3`

This command sets the pen size. Big numbers make thicker lines.

ADD A TITLE

Here's how to title your project:

1. **On the toolbar, click the Create a Text Box button.**
2. **Click in the workspace and drag the mouse to draw a rectangle.**

   A text1 text box appears in the workspace.

3. **Click and type** Quick Draw **inside the text box.**
4. **Select (highlight) the text inside the text box.**
5. **From the menu bar, choose Text. Then select Font, Size, Style, and Color to format your title.**

To resize a text box, right-click (Windows) or Control-click (Mac) the box and pull on the sizing dots.

6 **Make the text box transparent. Right-click (Windows) or Control-click (Mac) inside the title text box and select Transparent from the pop-up menu. This way, you see only text, not the box.**

7 **Click your title text and drag it where you would like to put the title.**

You can edit text only when the text box is opaque (not transparent). To change a text box from transparent to opaque, right-click (Windows) or Control-click (Mac) the text and select Opaque from the pop-up menu.

PUT COMMANDS TOGETHER

To put commands together, type a short sequence of commands in the Command Center. This example shows ten commands.

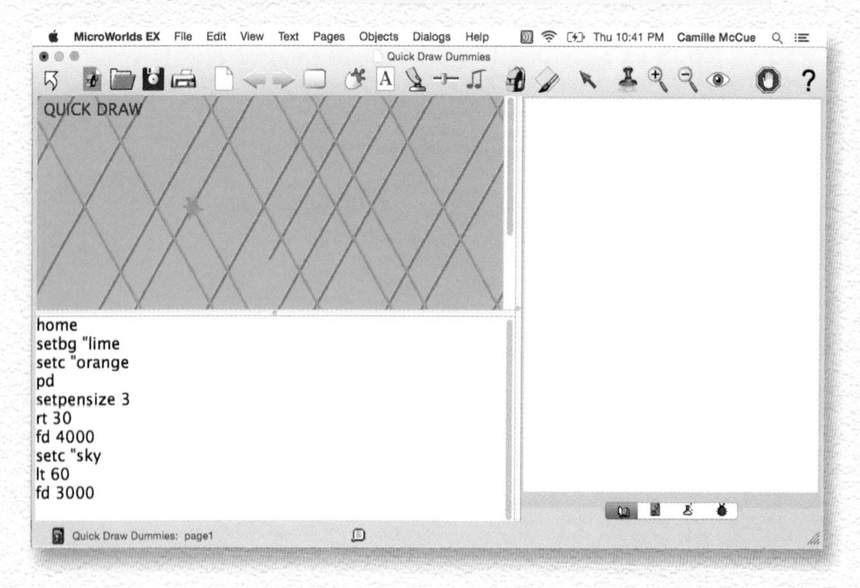

You can adjust the areas of the MicroWorlds EX interface by grabbing any divider line and pulling it to make the areas bigger or smaller.

One basic idea in coding is that commands are executed sequentially *(in order) until a* loop *or* branch *is reached. We'll look more closely at these three paths in Project 5!*

CREATE BUTTONS

The Command Center is a good place to test out commands as you develop a program. But a real program or app needs a *graphical user interface* (also called a *GUI*) with buttons, pictures, and menus for people to use your computer program.

Instead of asking users to type in a command such as `setbg "lime`, give them a button to press!

Make a button for changing background color as follows:

1. **From the toolbar, click the Create a Button button and then click anywhere in the workspace.**
2. **In the Button dialog box, fill in the following information:**
   - Label: Type **Lime Back**
   - Instruction: Type **setbg "lime**
   - Leave everything else the same.

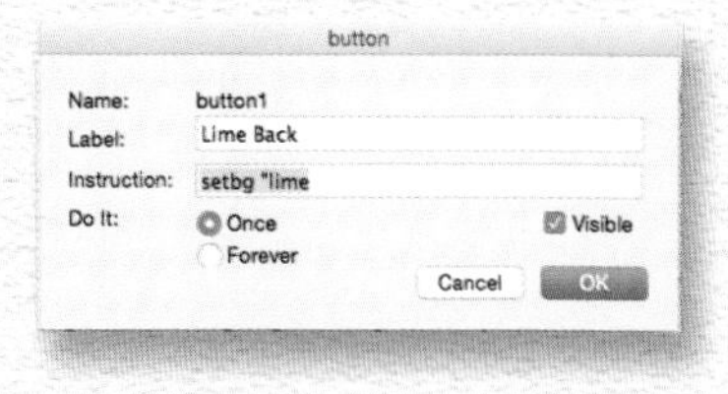

3. **Click OK.**

   The Lime Back button is added to the workspace.
4. **Drag the button to anywhere you want.**

To resize a button, right-click (Windows) or Control-click (Mac) the button and pull on the sizing dots.

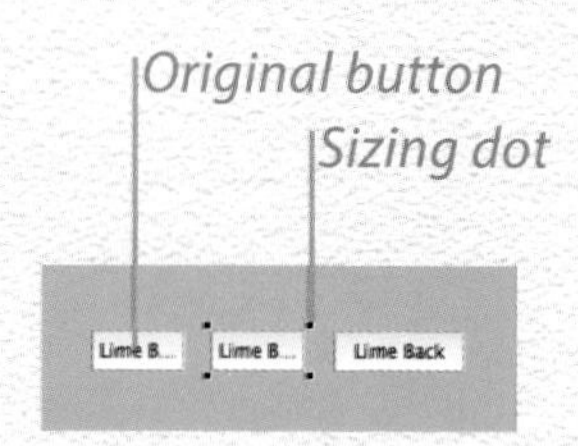

On some of the buttons, set the *Do It* radio button to Forever in the Button dialog box. This makes the button command execute over and over (until you click the button again or click the Stop All button on the toolbar). Then press more than one button to make many commands run at the same time!

CLEAN

Erase your workspace by typing the `clean` command at the Command Center. Graphics are cleaned off, but the turtle stays.

Make more buttons using the commands you know so far! Your Quick Draw looks something like this:

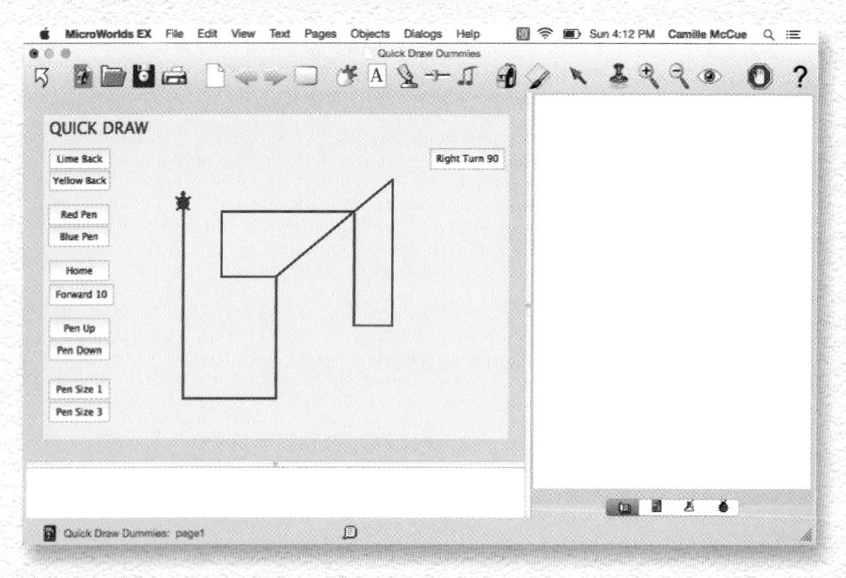

To delete a turtle, right-click (Windows) or Control-click (Mac) the turtle and select Delete from the pop-up menu.

WRITE PROCEDURES

A *procedure* is a new command you create. A procedure is really just a shortcut for a list of commands.

Here is how to make a procedure to draw a square that is 30 steps on a side:

1. **Press the Procedures tab (found in the lower-right corner of the MicroWorlds EX window).**

2. **Type the code at right.**

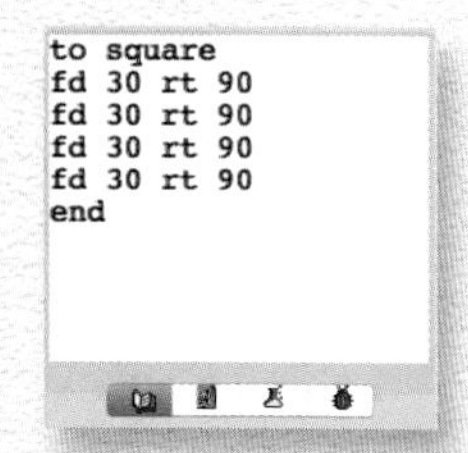

A new procedure starts with `to` followed by the name of the procedure. Do *not* use spaces in the name of the procedure. The last line of a new procedure is `end`.

Try out your new `square` procedure by typing it into the Command Center or making a button to run it.

If you forget to conclude with `end` *in your procedure, the Command Center gives an error message like the one shown here. If you see an error message, simply edit your procedure and test it again until it runs.*

```
square
I don't know how to square
```

3. **A key idea when writing computer code is keeping code *efficient*, meaning as simple as possible. Because the `square` procedure runs the same command (`fd 30 rt 90`) four times, a more efficient way to write the code**

is to use the `repeat` command. In the Procedure pane, edit your `square` procedure to look like this:

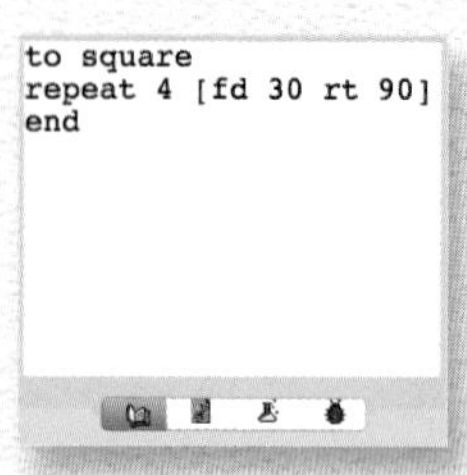

The `repeat` number tells how many repetitions to do. The repeated commands go inside square brackets: `[fd 30 rt 90]`.

Drag the Square button to a position where it doesn't block the artwork the user will be making. Then test the button a few times, moving the turtle to different locations as you draw squares.

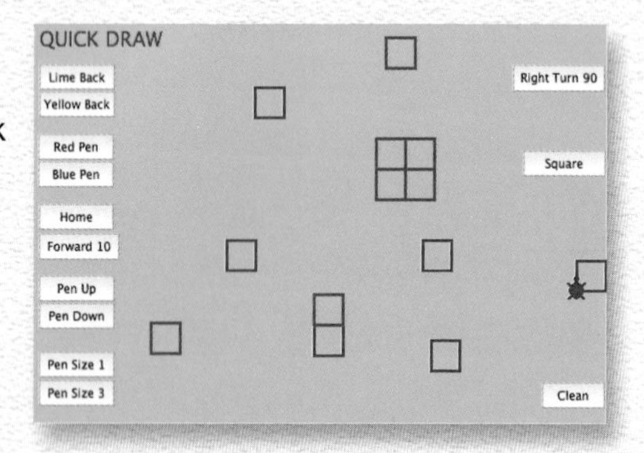

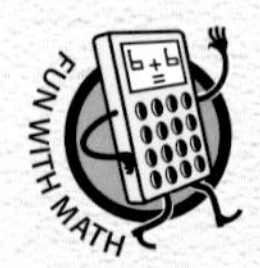

A square can be constructed using four right turns or four left turns, so the `square` *procedure could use an* `lt` *instead of an* `rt` *command!*

Try writing procedures and buttons to make other shapes, or polygons. A triangle has 3 sides and a turn angle of 120. An octagon has 8 sides and a turn angle of 45.

Even though a circle doesn't have sides (and isn't a polygon), you can draw a shape that looks like a circle using 360 sides and a turn angle of 1. (When making a circle, use a small `fd` value or else your circle will spill over the edges.) Do you see a multiplication pattern here?

DESIGN YOUR GUI

Arrange the buttons in the workspace to complete your Quick Draw. Think carefully about the graphical user interface (GUI). The user will expect buttons and other parts of the interface to be organized in an easy-to-understand layout.

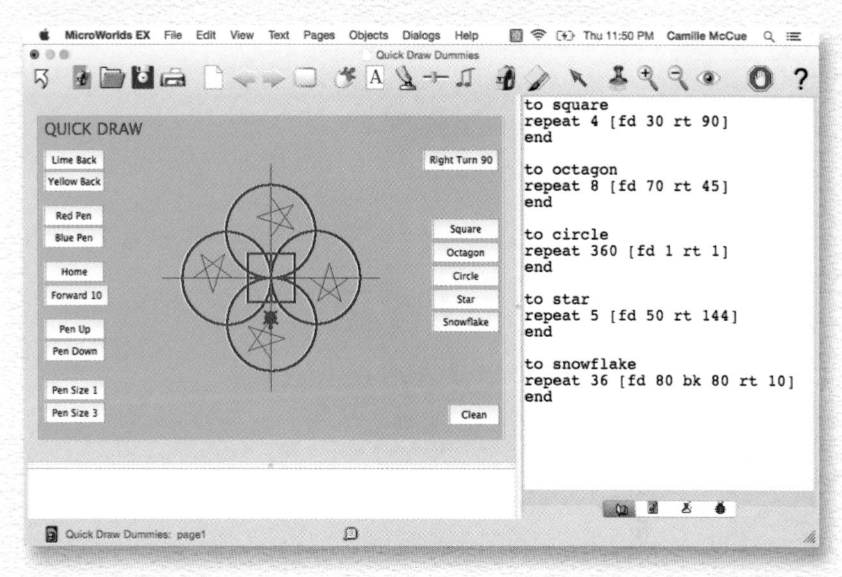

Procedures you create in a project exist only in that project — they can only be used in other projects if you copy and paste them into the new project.

ENHANCE YOUR APP

Add fun new features to your app! Add lots of new buttons for background colors and pen colors. Try making a random color button such as `setc random 140` (there are 140 colors in the MicroWorlds EX color palette). Make new polygons! Try shapes such a pentagon using `repeat 5 [fd 100 rt 72]`. Nest procedures by putting one inside of another.

For example, try this sequence of commands in the Command Center.

```
setbg "black repeat 8 [fd 70 snowflake
setc random 140 rt 45]
```

If you want a command sequence, name it and add it to the Procedures pane, then make a button for it!

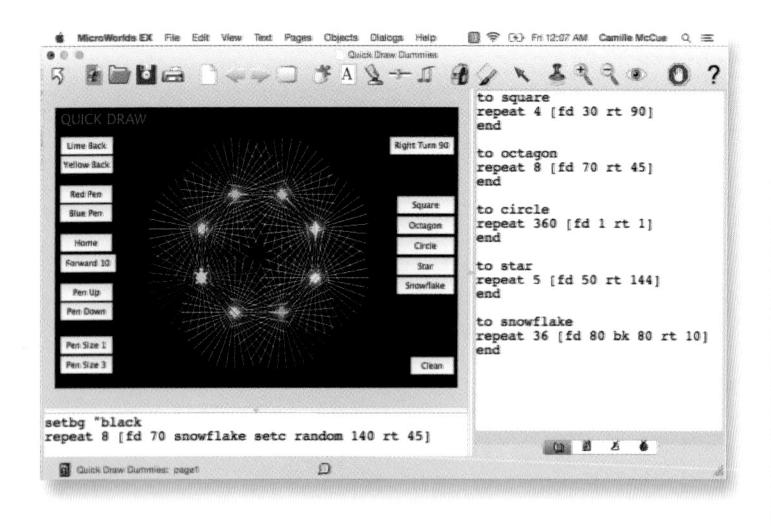

SAVE, TEST, AND DEBUG

Choose File and then choose Save Project from the menu bar to save your project.

Test each button in your Quick Draw to make sure it works. If it doesn't, look for error messages in the Command Center — they provide clues about how to correct your code. If you find a *bug,* meaning a problem with your code, look at each line of code carefully and check for misspelled primitives and missing quotes. Also, check that new procedures begin with `to` and end with `end`.

If a button is executing Forever, you can always stop execution by clicking the Stop All button on the MicroWorlds EX toolbar.

Once finished, play with the Quick Draw app and ask friends to play with it, too!

LAST LOOK ... BIG IDEAS IN CODING

In Quick Draw, you designed and coded a fun drawing tool, complete with an easy-to-use graphical user interface. You explored many concepts that you'll use again and again as you gain experience coding. On the next page is one last look at the key codes and ideas in Quick Draw:

BIG IDEAS IN CODING

setbg and setc
SETS COLORS

home
SENDS OBJECT TO CENTER AT (0,0)

fd, bk, rt, lt
COMMANDS FOR MOVING AN OBJECT AND TURNING IT

to procedurename… end
DEFINES A PROCEDURE

repeat
DRAWS A SIDE OF A SHAPE AND THEN TURNS... DOES THIS MANY TIMES TO MAKE A COMPLETE SHAPE

OBJECT
AN OBJECT CAN DRAW OR BE A CHARACTER IN GAMES, MODELS.

GUI
THESE INTERFACES PRESENT TEXT AND BUTTONS TO THE USER.

PROCEDURES
PUT COMMANDS TOGETHER TO DO NEW THINGS.

EFFICIENCY
DON'T REWRITE THE SAME CODE OVER AND OVER... USE A LOOP!

PROJECT 3 COIN FLIPPER

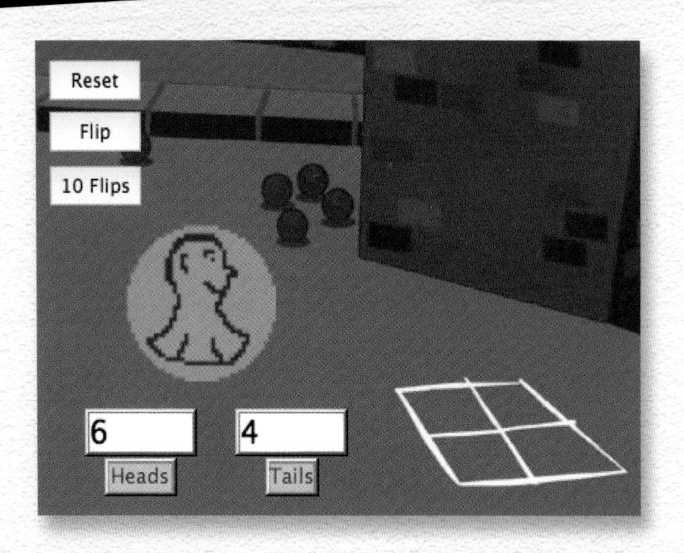

HAVE YOU EVER FLIPPED A COIN TO DECIDE SOMETHING ON THE SCHOOL PLAYGROUND? There are two outcomes when flipping a coin — heads or tails. On any flip, each side has a 50% chance of showing. Code this coin flipper to flip a virtual coin, and then add code to flip the coin many times!

BRAINSTORM

A *simulation* is a pretend version of a real event. Simulations can help you understand something faster or easier than watching real-world events. In this project, you click a button to make a pretend coin flip. Then, using the `repeat` command, you can simulate many coin flips, like 10 flips, or more! What other real-world events can you simulate?

GAME PLAN

Per this game plan for making the Coin Flipper simulation, we need to create graphics and write code. Keep this plan in mind as you work through the steps.

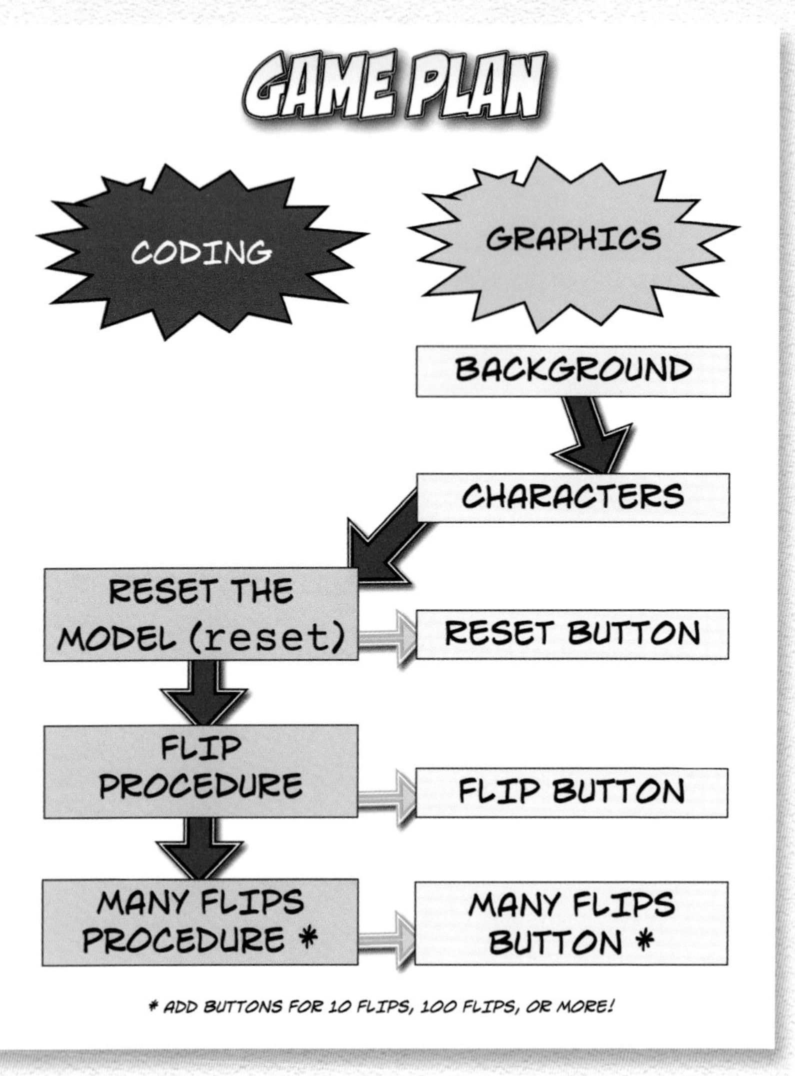

START A NEW PROJECT

Begin Coin Flipper by starting a new project:

1. **Start MicroWorlds EX.**
2. **On the yellow MicroWorlds EX startup screen, select Free Mode.**

   A new project opens.

3. **From the menu bar, choose File and then choose Web Player.**

   The *workspace* appears.

APPLY A BACKGROUND

We're flipping a coin at school, so let's apply a recess playground background to the simulation:

1. **From the toolbar, click the Hide/Show Painting/Clipart button.**

   The Painting/Clipart palette opens.

2. **Click the Backgrounds button to show the backgrounds.**
3. **Click the playground background, and then click in the workspace to apply the background image.**
4. **Right-click (Windows) or Control-click (Mac) the background image. From the pop-up menu, select Stamp Full Page.**

   The image fills the entire workspace.

5. **Close the Painting/Clipart palette.**

ADD A TURTLE

The simulation has only one turtle object. The turtle will become the coin.

1. **On the toolbar, click the Create a Turtle button.**
2. **Click in the workspace. A turtle appears.**

   Drag the turtle to a position in the playground.

RESIZE THE TURTLE

The turtle object has a starting, or *default*, size of 40. This is a little small. Increase the size of the turtle, by typing **setsize 100** in the Command Center and pressing Enter (Windows) or Return (Mac).

PAINTING BACKGROUNDS AND SHAPES

The Painting/Clipart palette has tools for drawing and painting in the workspace. The Shape Editor works the same way for making new shapes for turtles. Open the Painting/Clipart palette by clicking the Hide/Show Painting/Clipart button on the toolbar. To see the painting tools, click the button in the upper-left corner of the palette.

The row of small buttons includes the drawing and painting tools: Pencil for free-form drawing; Pen for lines; Paint Can for fills; Spray; Rectangle; Filled Rectangle; Oval; Filled Oval; Selector for selecting rectangular regions; Lasso for selecting free-form areas; Color Picker for sampling a color; Eraser; and Undo.

Below the painting tools are the drawing brush tips. Each brush is a different shape, size, fade, and style.

The middle of the palette shows the paint colors. Each color has a number from 0 to 139. Each column of colors is a family. Grays are in the first family, followed by reds, and so on. Below the color families is the Opacity slider. Set at 100%, a selected color is opaque (not see-through). Set at 0%, a color is transparent (see-through). The bottom of the palette consists of textures.

CREATE COIN SHAPES

The turtle doesn't have to look like a turtle. It can look like a coin. At each flip, the turtle will wear a shape showing whether it is heads or tails. Create shapes using these steps:

1. **Click the project's Shapes tab (located in the lower-right corner of the window).**
2. **On the Shapes pane, double-click a shape spot.**

   The Shape Editor opens.
3. **Use the drawing tools in the Shape Editor to draw a heads shape in any way you want!**
4. **Name the shape H (in the empty white field at the top of the Shape Editor) and then click OK.**

   The Shape Editor closes, and the H shape appears in the Shapes pane.

5. **Repeat Steps 2–4 to create a tails shape.**

6 Name this shape T at the top of the Shape Editor and then click OK.

The Shape Editor closes, and the T shape appears in the Shapes pane.

7 Click either the H or T shape in the Shapes pane and then move into the workspace and click the turtle.

The turtle now wears the shape.

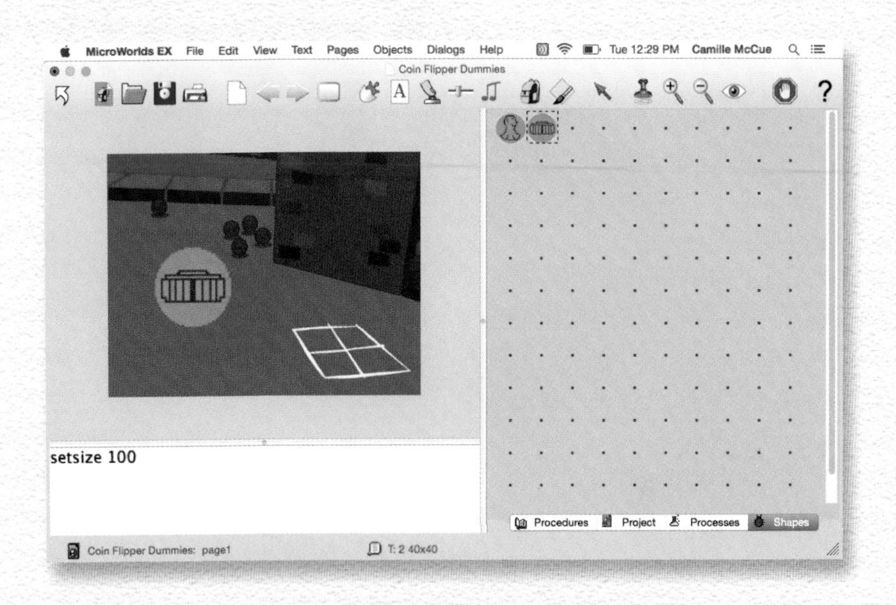

If you accidentally drop the shape onto the background instead of the turtle, just right-click (Windows) or Control-click (Mac) the shape and select Remove from the pop-up menu.

As you program, your mouse pointer will sometimes appear as a cursor (in places where you can type), sometimes as a regular pointer (for dragging a turtle, button, or other element), and sometimes as a hand for placing shapes in the workspace. You can always change the mouse back to a pointer by clicking the Regular Pointer button.

CREATE COUNTERS

The Coin Flipper simulation needs a way to show the turtle change each time a coin is flipped. It also needs variables to count how many total heads and how many total tails appear after many flips.

Variables *are quantities that can have different values at different times.*

Create a *counting variable* or *counter* to count the total number of heads as follows:

1 From the toolbar, click the Create a Text Box button; move into the workspace and drag out a rectangle for the text box.

Instead of showing a title, this text box will show a variable value.

2 In the Text dialog box, fill in the following information:

- Name: Type **Heads**.
- Leave everything else the same.

3 Click OK.

The text box label now shows Heads.

4 Drag the text box to anywhere you want.

5 If you need to edit the text box, click the Eye Tool on the toolbar and then click the text box.

6 Repeat Steps 1–5 to make a tails counting variable and a workspace similar to this:

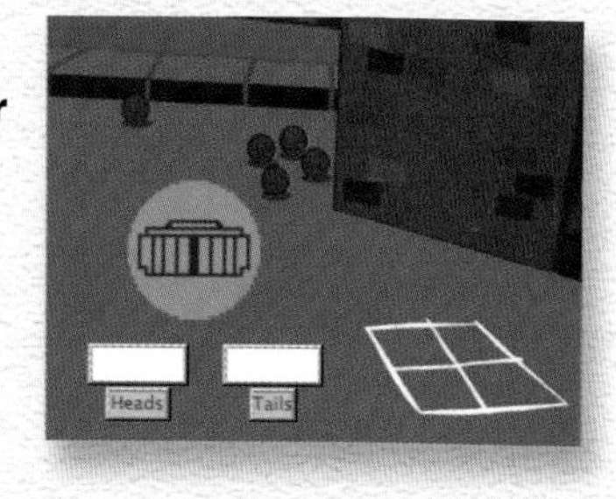

Don't get confused between the names of the shapes (`H` *and* `T`*) and the names of the counting variables (*`Heads` *and* `Tails`*).*

To resize a text box, Ctrl-click (Windows) or Command-click (Mac) the button and pull on the sizing dots.

Text boxes used as variables must remain opaque for the variable values to change. Don't make them transparent!

WRITE A RESET PROCEDURE

Like any simulation, Coin Flipper needs a starting point. You need a procedure to reset the model. The `reset` procedure starts when the number of flips is zero.

Write a `reset` procedure and create a button to execute it:

1 Click the project's Procedures tab (located in the lower-right corner of the window).

2 Type the `reset` procedure as shown:

```
to reset
setheads 0
settails 0
end
```

This sets the starting value of the `heads` and `tails` variables to zero. Now that you have written the `reset` procedure, MicroWorlds EX recognizes it as a new command that you can use!

CREATE A RESET BUTTON

Make a button to run the `reset` procedure:

1 From the toolbar, click the Create a Button button, and then click anywhere in the workspace.

2 In the Button dialog box, fill in the following information:

- Label: Type **Reset**
- Instruction: Type **reset**
- Leave everything else the same.

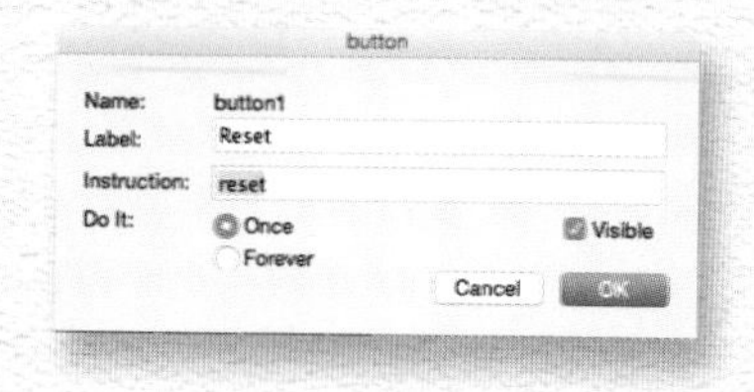

3 Click OK.

The Reset button is added to the workspace.

4 Drag the button to anywhere you want.

To resize a button, Ctrl-click (Windows) or Command-click (Mac) the button and pull on the sizing dots.

5 Test your Reset button by clicking it. A zero should appear in the Heads text box, and a zero should appear in the Tails text box.

In programming, you will often need to set the starting or initial *value of a variable. That's because you must know how much of a quantity you have initially (at the beginning) so that you can figure out how much you end up with when you add to the quantity, or subtract from the quantity.*

Some programming languages are picky about whether you use a capital letter or a lowercase letter. MicroWorlds EX does not care.

WRITE A FLIP PROCEDURE

When flipping a coin, you know that *if* you see an H shape (a person's head) *then* you have flipped a head. And, *if* you see a T shape (a building) *then* you have flipped a tail. You will create these same `if-then` commands in your program code.

Write a procedure to flip the coin:

In the Procedures pane, type the `flip` procedure as shown:

```
to flip
setshape pick [H T]
if shape = "H [setheads Heads + 1]
if shape = "T [settails Tails + 1]
end
```

This procedure sets the shape put onto the coin randomly using `pick`. The two possible shapes are `H` and `T`. Each shape has a 50% chance of appearing.

The `flip` procedure then uses two `if-then` conditional statements:

- The first conditional says that if the `H` shape is picked, then add `1` to the current value of the `Heads` variable.
- The second conditional says that if the `T` shape is picked, then add `1` to the current value of the `Tails` variable.

Here, the `Heads` variable and the `Tails` variable are counters for the total number of girls and the total number of boys.

`If-then` *conditionals are logic statements that are common in coding. The general form is* `if condition then consequence`.

CREATE A FLIP BUTTON

Make a button to run the `flip` procedure:

1. **From the toolbar, click the Create a Button button, and then click anywhere in the workspace.**
2. **In the Button dialog box, fill in the following information:**
   - Label: Type **Flip**
   - Instruction: Type **flip**
   - Leave everything else the same.
3. **Click OK.**

   The Flip button is added to the workspace.
4. **Drag the button to a position near the Reset button.**
5. **Test your Flip button by clicking it. The shape worn by the coin turtle object should change. The associated `Heads` or `Tails` variable value should increase by 1.**
6. **If you need to edit the button, click the Eye Tool on the toolbar and then click the button.**

CREATE MANY FLIPS PROCEDURES AND BUTTONS

After you make both the `reset` procedure and the `flip` procedure, you can put them together in new ways. You can combine these two procedures with a `repeat` command to make the coin many times, very fast. How many heads and how many tails do you think the simulation will make for ten flips?

A frequency distribution *shows how many of each outcome there is in a group. The group is called a sample or a* population.

The `repeat` *command is a type of* loop. *Loops are common in programming because they let you write a command once and then run it over and over again.*

1 In the Procedures pane, type the `10flips` procedure as shown:

```
to 10flips
reset
repeat 10 [flip] wait 1
end
```

This allows you to flip the coin ten times, really fast — and count the total number of heads and the total number of tails. The `wait 1` command is there to slow down the flipping so you can see the shape change on each flip.

Both the `reset` *procedure and the* `flip` *procedure are nested in the* `10flips` *procedure.*

2 From the toolbar, click the Create a Button button, and then click anywhere in the workspace.

3 In the Button dialog box, fill in the following information:

- Label: Type **10 Flips**
- Instruction: Type **10flips**
- Leave everything else the same.

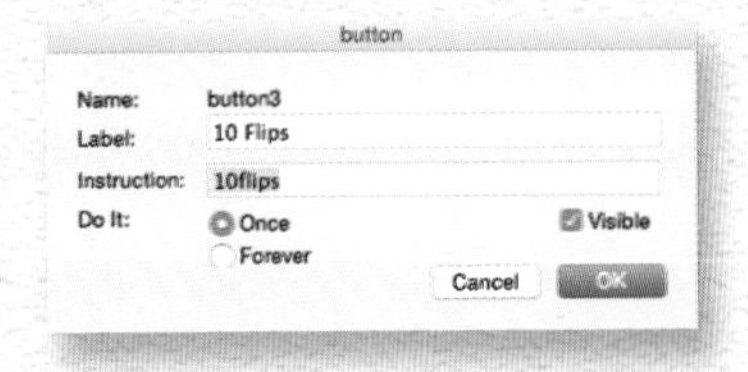

Note that the Label and Instruction do not have to show the same text; just be sure that the Instruction does not have spaces in it.

4 Click OK.

The 10 Flips button is added to the workspace.

5 Drag the button to a position near the other buttons.

6 Test your 10 Flips button by clicking it. The counters should reset to `0`. Then, the shape worn by the coin turtle object should change each time the nested `flip` procedure executes, and the `Heads` and `Tails` variables should keep a running count of flip outcomes.

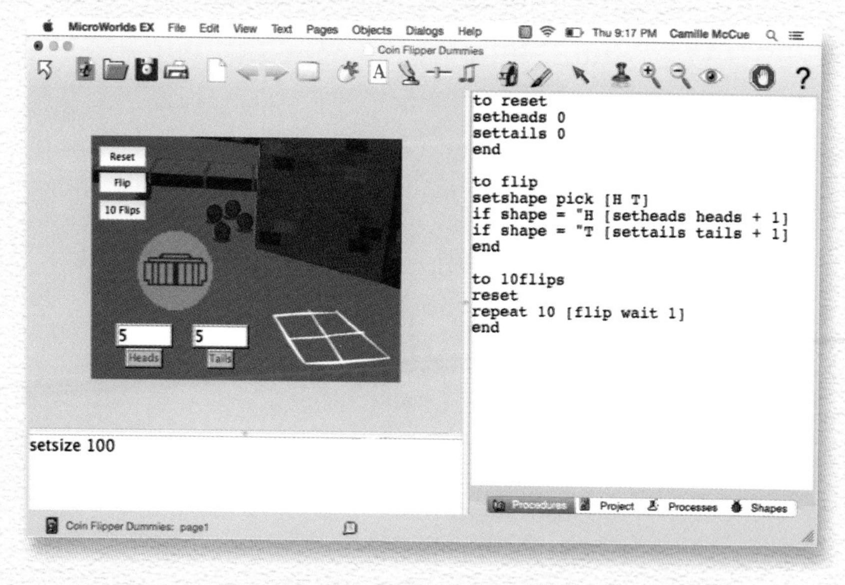

7 If you need to edit the button, click the Eye Tool on the toolbar and then click the button.

8 Repeat Steps 1–6 to make procedures and buttons for additional flip buttons.

Try 100 flips, or 1,000 flips!

SAVE, TEST, AND DEBUG

Choose File and then choose Save Project from the menu bar to save your project.

Test each button in your simulation to make sure it works. If it doesn't, look for error messages in the Command Center — they provide clues about how to correct your code. When you're finished, run the simulation several times and evaluate how well you believe it models the real world.

LAST LOOK ... BIG IDEAS IN CODING

This project had commands you will want to use in other MicroWorlds EX projects. It also had many big ideas that are found in most programming languages. Keep these in mind as you work on new projects!

ENHANCE YOUR SIMULATION

Now that you know how to build the basic procedures and buttons in the Coin Flipper simulation, you may want to enhance your project! Can you create coin shapes based on real currency in other countries? What about making a button to flip the coin a thousand times?

Can you extend the ideas in this project to create a dice roller? Or — for something really challenging — can you create a "Yahtzee" game that rolls five dice at the same time? (Hint: You will need to make five turtle objects and six shapes, and you will need the `everyone` command.)

BIG IDEAS IN CODING

pick
MAKE A RANDOM HEAD OR TAIL

setsize
SHRINK OR GROW A COIN

repeat
FLIP THE COIN MANY TIMES

RANDOM
REAL EVENTS ARE RANDOM. A COIN CAN BE A HEAD OR TAIL.

LOOP
A LOOP RUNS A PIECE OF CODE OVER AND OVER.

VARIABLE
SOMETHING THAT CAN BE DIFFERENT NUMBERS, LIKE A COUNTER.

CONDITIONAL
COMMAND THAT RUNS SOME CODE ONLY WHEN TRUE.

PROJECT 4 SPACE RACE

IN THIS PROJECT, YOU CREATE A FUN GAME THAT CHALLENGES PLAYERS TO CONQUER THE SPACE RACE! What's an astronaut to do when trying to spacewalk through rocket ships, asteroids, and UFOs to reach home?

BRAINSTORM

Choose any main character and obstacles you want … a starfish trying to get away from hungry sea life … a student moving through a busy hallway to reach her locker … or a parachutist avoiding clouds as he floats down to Earth.

GAME PLAN

Here's the game plan for building the Space Race game. The game needs both graphics and code. Keep this plan in mind as you work through the steps. Remember, this is your plan for creating the game, not a flow chart of game operation.

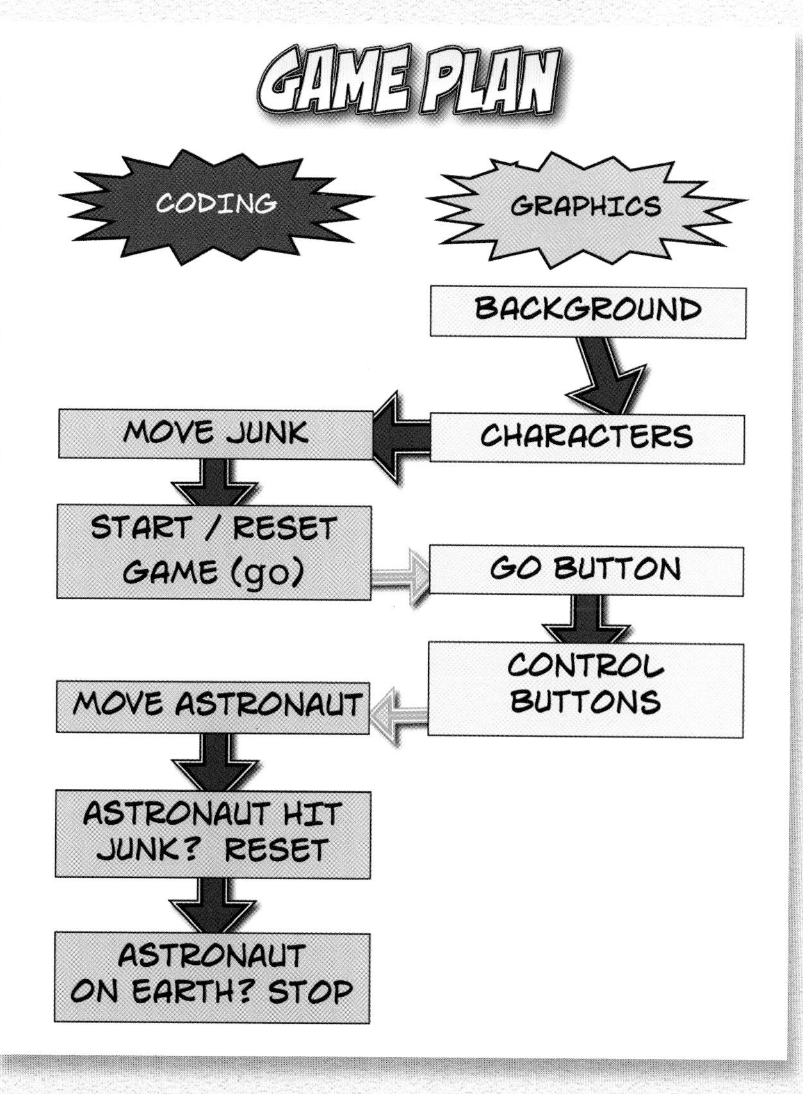

START A NEW PROJECT

Begin Space Race by starting a new project:

1. **Start MicroWorlds EX.**
2. **On the yellow MicroWorlds EX startup screen, select Free Mode.**

   A new project opens.

3. **Type** newprojectsize [400 600] **in the Command Center.**

   This creates a workspace similar to the screen of a mobile phone.

APPLY A BACKGROUND

Apply a space and planetary background to the game:

1. **From the toolbar, click the Hide/Show Painting/Clipart button.**

   The Painting/Clipart palette opens.

2. **Click the Backgrounds button to show the backgrounds.**
3. **Click the space and planet background, and then click in the workspace to apply the background image.**
4. **Right-click (Windows) or Control-click (Mac) the background image. From the pop-up menu, select Stamp Full Page.**

   The image fills the entire workspace.

5 **Leave the Painting/Clipart palette open; you will need this again when you create your astronaut and space junk characters.**

ADD AN ASTRONAUT

The game has many turtle objects. The player controls a turtle object that looks like an astronaut. Let's make the astronaut:

1 **On the toolbar, click the Create a Turtle button.**

2 **Click in the workspace. A turtle appears.**

Drag the turtle to the bottom of the screen.

3 **In the Painting/Clipart palette, click the Singles.**

4 **Scroll to find the astronaut shape. Click it and then move into the workspace and click the turtle.**

The turtle now wears the astronaut shape.

If you accidentally click somewhere other than the turtle, the astronaut shape will appear on the background — just right-click (Windows) or Control-click (Mac) the shape and select Remove from the pop-up menu to get rid of it.

The astronaut looks a little large! Don't worry about changing his size now. You will be making more turtle objects and you will change the size of all of them with one command a little later.

NAME THE ASTRONAUT

There will be many turtle objects in this game, but you only have to name one. The astronaut turtle needs a name because it needs to know when you are giving special commands only to it.

1 On the toolbar, click the Eye Tool button and then click the turtle.

The turtle backpack opens.

The turtle backpack is like your backpack. It contains all the turtle's important stuff. There are tabs at the bottom of the backpack window that organize the backpack into sections. The tabs you will use are State (which has information) and Rules (which has instructions for the turtle to follow).

2 At the State tab, click the Edit button next to the Name field.

3 In the Name dialog box that appears, type astronaut **in the Name field.**

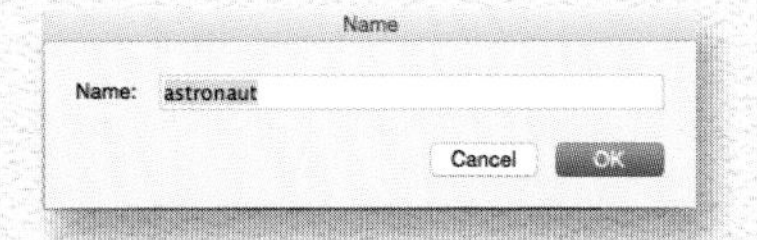

4 Click OK to close the Name dialog box, but leave the backpack open at the State tab; you will need it in the next section.

If you hover over a turtle with your mouse for a few seconds, its name will appear.

PUT ASTRONAUT AT START POSITION

Drag the astronaut turtle to the bottom of the workspace. You need to know where this position is so you can put the astronaut here at the start of the game. The astronaut also needs to go to this position after hitting a piece of space junk so that it can start the game over. Find the position, or *coordinates*, of the astronaut as follows:

1. **At the State tab of the astronaut turtle backpack, note the Xcor — the x-coordinate — of this position and write it down.**
2. **At the State tab of the astronaut turtle backpack, note the Ycor — the y-coordinate — of this position and write it down.**
3. **Close the astronaut backpack.**

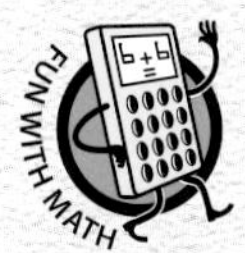

Positions in two dimensions (2D) can be written as (x-coordinate, y-coordinate). *For example: (0, –255).*

CREATE SPACE JUNK CHARACTERS

Space junk characters are turtle objects wearing a variety of shapes. Follow these steps to create the space junk:

1. **On the toolbar, click the Create a Turtle button. Move into the workspace and click to hatch a turtle. Drag this "space traffic" into a position between the astronaut and Earth.**

2. **Give the turtle a space junk shape to wear. In the Painting/Clipart palette, click the Singles button. Click a shape (a UFO, a robot, or an asteroid) and then move into the workspace and click the turtle.**

   The turtle now wears the space junk shape.

3 Set the turtle Heading (the direction it will move when animated) to match the direction in which the shape is pointing. On the Toolbar, click the Eye Tool button and then click the turtle; the turtle backpack opens. At the State tab of the space junk turtle backpack, type a number for the Heading.

For east, the heading is 90. For west, the heading is 270. For the robot example, the heading is set to 270.

A circle has 360 degrees. In MicroWorlds EX, north is 0 degrees, and measurement around the circle is in the clockwise direction.

4 Close the backpack.

5 Repeat Steps 1–4 to create more space junk!

Be sure to make some junk with headings pointing east and other junk with headings pointing west.

ANIMATE THE SPACE JUNK

Right-click (Windows) or Control-click (Mac) a space junk turtle and select Animate from the pop-up menu to make it move! Repeat for all the space junk turtles.

To stop turtles from moving, just press the Stop button at the Toolbar.

RESIZE THE TURTLES

All the turtle objects have a starting, or *default*, size of 40. But you probably noticed all the turtles are too big for your game. Shrink the turtles by typing **everyone [setsize 25]** in the Command Center and pressing Enter (Windows) or Return (Mac).

CONTROL THE ASTRONAUT

Follow these steps to create four buttons — N, E, S, and W — for moving the astronaut north, east, south, and west:

1. **First, create a button to point the astronaut turtle north. On the toolbar, click the Create a Button button. Then click the workspace anywhere.**

2. **In the Button dialog box, fill in the following information:**

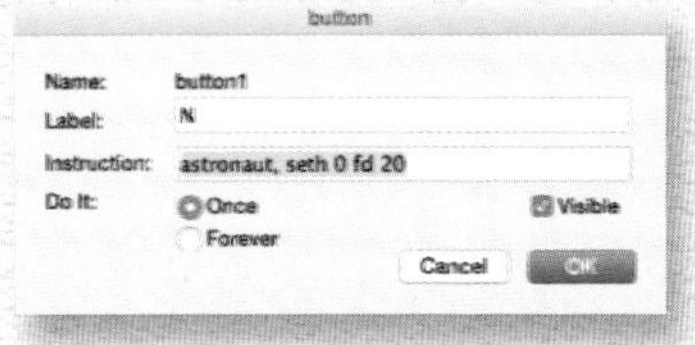

   » Label: Type **N** (for north) in the Label field to name the button.

   » Instruction: Type **astronaut, seth 0 fd 20** in the Instruction field. Here's what the instruction does: The command `astronaut,` (including the comma) says, "I'm speaking only to the astronaut." The command `seth 0` tells the astronaut to set its heading to 0, meaning to point north. The `fd 20` command moves forward 20 pixels.

   » Leave everything else the same.

3. **Click OK to close the Button dialog box.**

   The N button is added to the workspace.

4. **Drag the button to the lower-left corner of the workspace.**

5. **Test the N button by clicking it.**

   The astronaut should move a small distance in the north direction.

6. **Repeat Steps 1–5 to create and test one button each for moving the astronaut E (east), S (south), and W (west). Here's a little help for writing the instruction for each direction.**

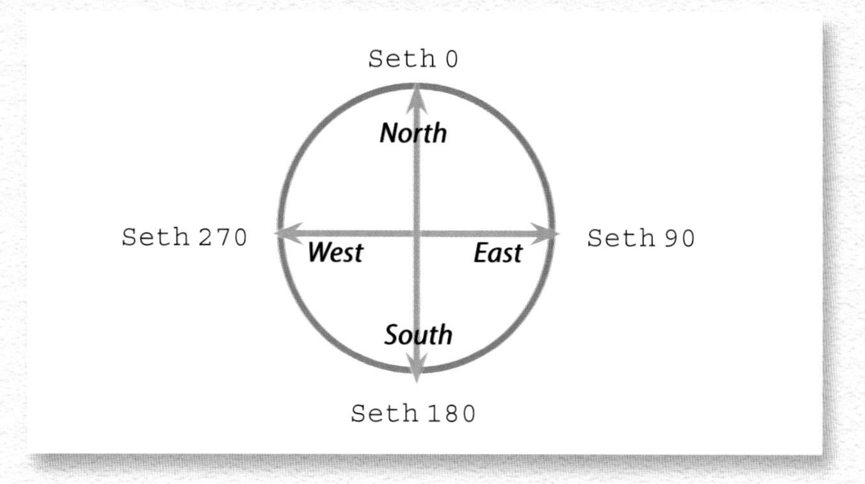

You may need to resize buttons to fit your game layout better. Ctrl-click (Windows) or Command-click (Mac) a button to summon sizing dots. Click and drag any of the dots to resize the button.

7 Arrange your N, E, S, and W buttons to match real compass headings.

Arrange player/user controls such as buttons in a clear and understandable layout. Your graphical user interface, or GUI, should allow the player/user to operate your app easily!

Freeze your astronaut turtle and your space junk turtles to prevent the player from clicking them and moving them during the game. Right-click (Windows) or Control-click (Mac) each turtle and then select Freeze from the pop-up menu.

WRITE A GO PROCEDURE

Your game will use a go procedure to set the astronaut to its starting position, and begin the game action.

On the project's Procedures pane, write this go procedure:

```
to go
astronaut, setpos [0 -255]
everyone [clickon]
end
```

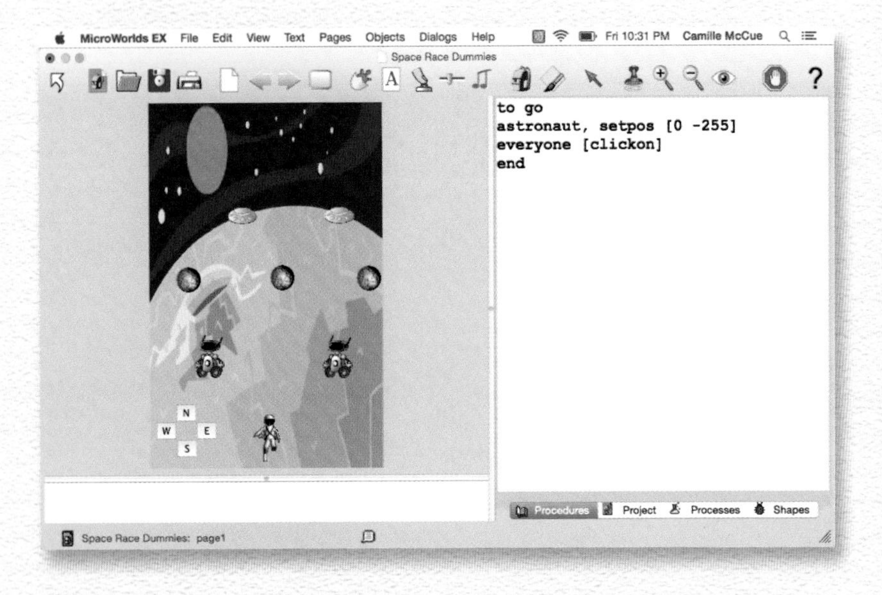

Replace [0 -255] with whatever Xcor and Ycor values you discovered in the earlier "Put Astronaut at Start Position" section.

MAKE A GO BUTTON

After you've written the go procedure, MicroWorlds EX now recognizes it as a new command that you can use. Follow these steps to create a button to run the procedure:

1. **On the toolbar, click the Create a Button button, and then click anywhere in the workspace.**

2 **In the Button dialog box, fill in the following fields:**

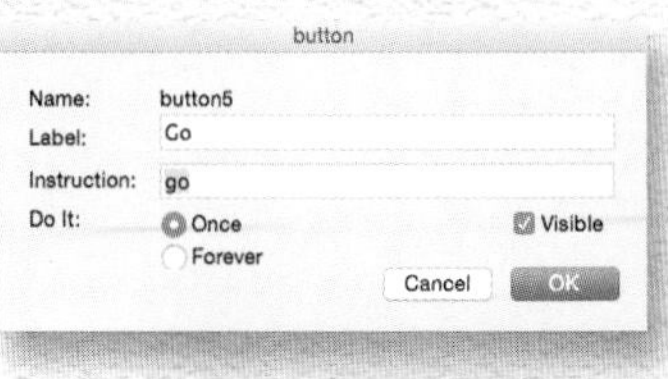

» Label: Type **Go** in the Label field to name the button.

» Instruction: Type **go**, which is the procedure that will run when this button is clicked.

» Leave everything else the same.

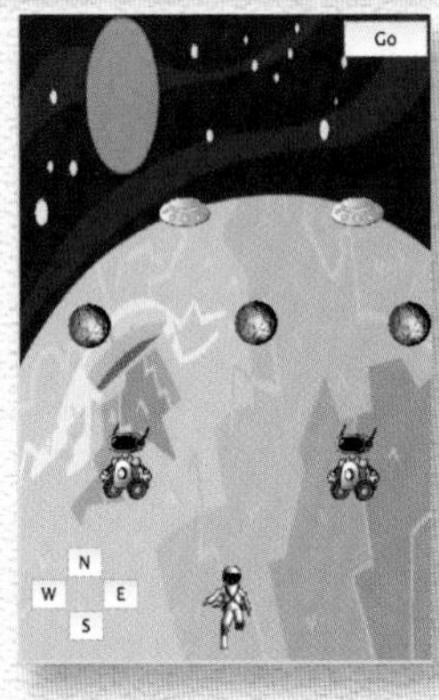

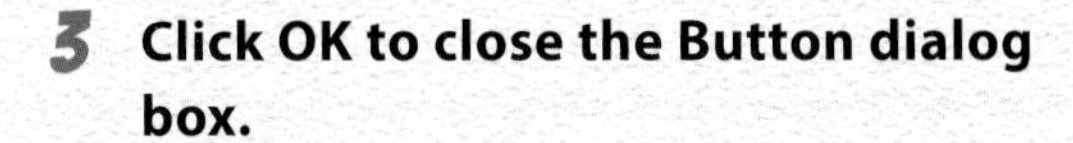

3 **Click OK to close the Button dialog box.**

The Go button is added to the workspace.

4 **Drag the button to the upper-right corner of the workspace.**

WATCH OUT FOR HITS!

Tell the `astronaut` turtle to state when it has been hit by space junk, and then restart the game.

1 **On the toolbar, click the Eye button. Then click the astronaut to open its backpack.**

2 **Press the Rules tab of the astronaut backpack.**

3 **In the OnTouching field, type** say [Hit!] go**.**

Now, whenever the astronaut collides with space junk during the game, the player will hear an audible "Hit!" Then the go procedure will run, starting the game action over.

4 **Close the backpack.**

A collision takes place when part of a turtle and part of another turtle are at the same coordinates. This is called coordinate convergence.

WIN THE GAME!

To win the game, the player must move the astronaut so that it touches the lime green color on planet Earth. Write commands to make the lime green color know when a turtle object is touching it:

1. **Right-click (Windows) or Control-click (Mac) a lime green continent region of Earth. From the pop-up menu that appears, select Edit lime.**

   The Instructions for: Lime dialog box appears and allows you to set the universal color conditional.

2. **In the Instructions for: Lime dialog box, fill in these fields:**

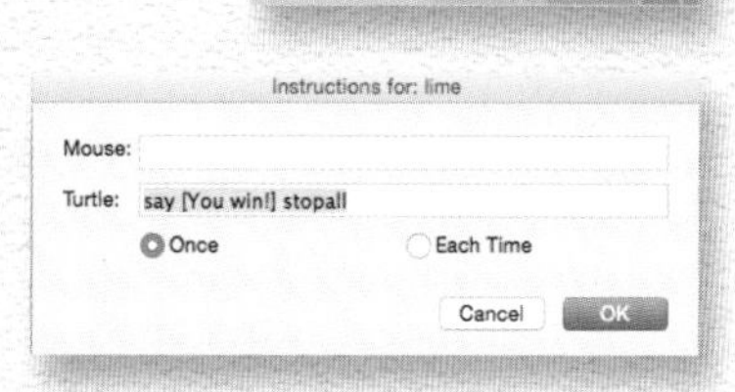

   » Mouse: Leave this field blank.

   » Turtle: In the Turtle field, type **say [You win!] stopall**.

   » Once: Select this radio button.

   This means that when a turtle is on the color lime, the player will hear an audible "You win!" Then the `stopall` procedure will run, stopping all game action. This occurs when the player succeeds in moving the astronaut to planet Earth without colliding with other objects.

3 Click OK to save your changes.

A universal color conditional *is a command that runs when any object touches the chosen color. Universal means that any turtle walking across the color (or mouse clicking the color) will cause the instructions to be executed. Because there is only one turtle object that might touch Earth — the astronaut — the win commands will only run if the astronaut wins the game.*

Universal color conditionals function only on background colors, not turtle colors and not colors in shapes worn by turtles.

 Press the Presentation Mode button on the Toolbar before having a friend play the game.

SAVE, TEST, AND DEBUG

Choose Save Project from File menu in the menu bar to save your game.

Test your game by playing it repeatedly. After you have worked out all the bugs, you can challenge friends to determine the Space Race champion!

LAST LOOK ... BIG IDEAS IN CODING

In Space Race, you created a functional game, just like those you see running on mobile devices! The concepts you learned here will be useful in other programming projects. Take one final look at some of these big ideas on the next page.

BIG IDEAS IN CODING

`seth`
SETS HEADINGS OF OBJECTS

`everyone [commands]`
ALL OBJECTS RUN COMMANDS

`setpos`
SETS OBJECT COORDINATES

CONSTANT MOTION
OBJECT MOVES A SMALL DISTANCE OVER AND OVER

POSITION
X AND Y COORDINATES TELL OBJECT POSITION

OBJECT NAMING
WITH MANY OBJECTS, AN OBJECT MUST KNOW ITS NAME TO COMMAND IT ALONE

COLLISION DETECTION
KNOWING WHEN TWO OBJECTS TOUCH

COLOR DETECTION
KNOWING WHEN AN OBJECT TOUCHES A COLOR

ENHANCE YOUR GAME

Consider enhancing your game with new features!

Some players figure out that by jumping backward, you can reach the goal and avoid the traffic. You can prevent cheats by getting rid of the ability to jump backward — just remove the south control button.

Or, you can add a color band at the bottom of the screen through which the astronaut can't move — like a black hole — and that announces his doom.

Get creative!

PROJECT 5 HA HA HEADLINES

IF YOU'VE PLAYED MAD LIBS, YOU'LL LOVE HA HA HEADLINES!

In this project, you discover how to handle and format text by building an app that creates a made-up news headline. A player will fill in the blanks with a few words — a candy bar name and an action verb — and then press a button to show and speak the news headline.

You do a lot of text formatting when writing computer programs! Making web pages means writing code in HTML — a language that mostly involves formatting text.

Knowing how to work with text is very important when writing a computer program and designing the user interface (UI).

BRAINSTORM

Besides news headlines, any story theme can be fun! You can use templates found in Mad Libs books, or use a real news or story selection in which you remove and replace some of the words. Think about using songs, recipes, or advertisements!

GAME PLAN

Like most projects, the game plan om the next page for making the headline includes creating simple graphics and writing code. Keep this plan in mind as you work through the steps.

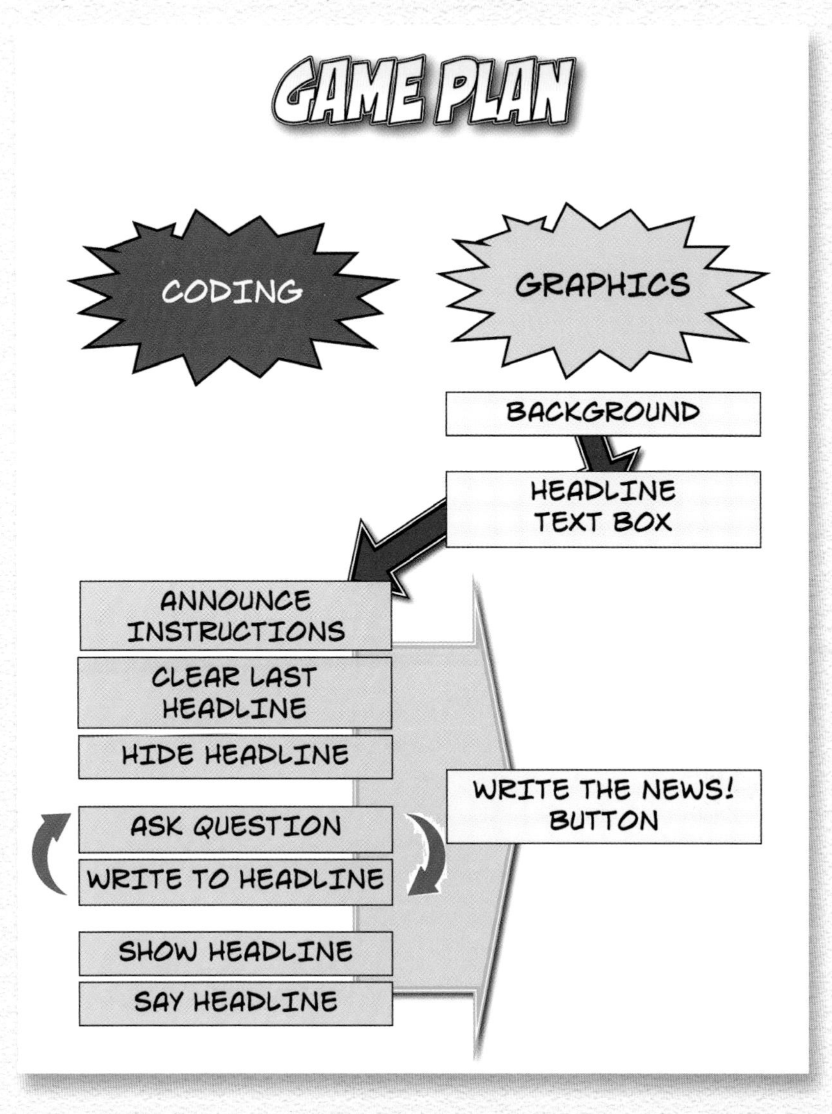

START A NEW PROJECT

Begin Ha Ha Headlines by starting a new project:

1. **Start MicroWorlds EX.**
2. **On the yellow MicroWorlds EX startup screen, select Free Mode.**

   A new project opens.
3. **From the menu bar, choose File and then choose New Project Size and select any project size you want.**

APPLY A BACKGROUND

We're creating a news headline, so let's apply a background that looks like something you see in a television news show:

1. **From the toolbar, click the Hide/Show Painting/Clipart button.**

   The Painting/Clipart palette opens.

2. **Click the Backgrounds button to show the backgrounds.**
3. **Click the TV News background, and then click in the workspace to apply the background image.**
4. **Right-click (Windows) or Control-click (Mac) the background image. From the pop-up menu, select Stamp Full Page.**

   The image fills the entire workspace.

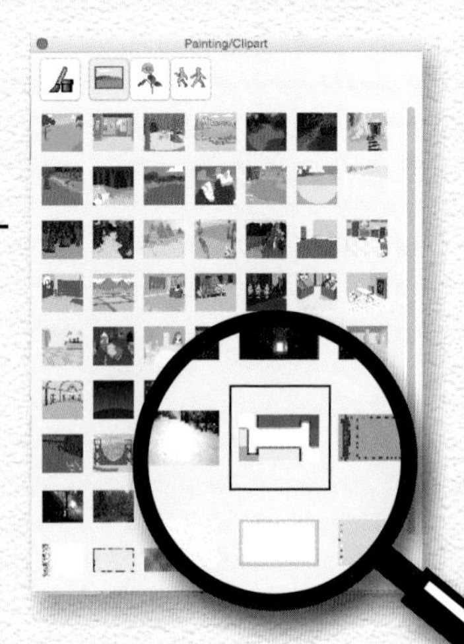

5 Close the Painting/Clipart palette.

MAKE A HEADLINE BOX

This project has one text box where the news headline will appear. Create it as follows:

1 On the toolbar, click the Create a Text Box button.

2 In the workspace, click the page and then drag to create a large rectangle for a text box.

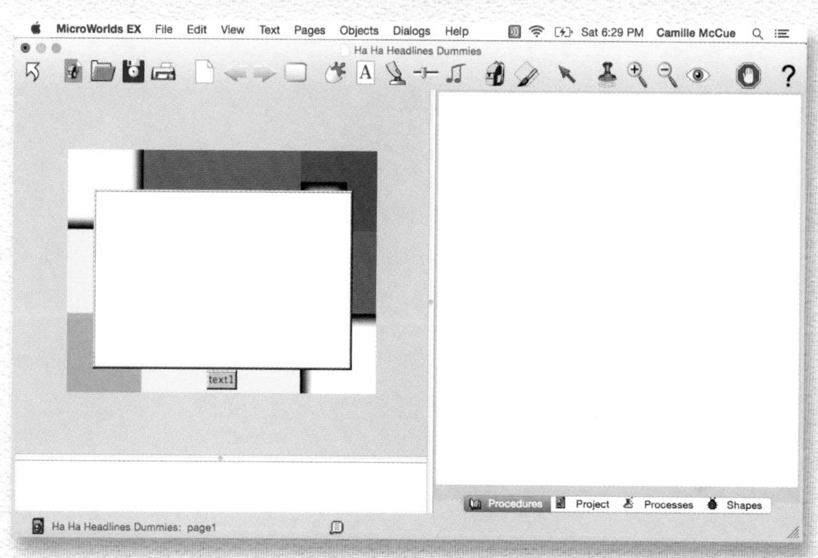

3 On the toolbar, click the Eye Tool button, and then click the text box. Select Edit from the pop-up menu.

A dialog box appears.

4 In the Text dialog box, fill in the following information:

- Name: Type **headline** to name the text box.
- Visible: Check this box.

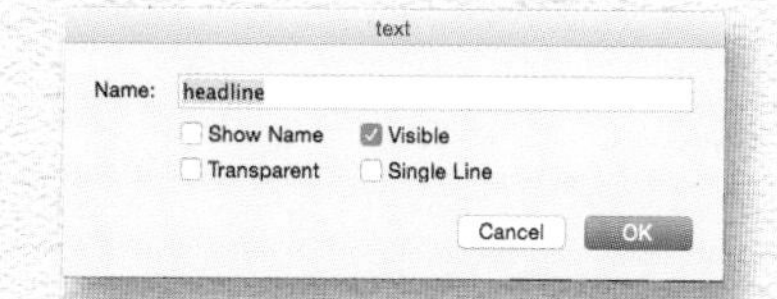

- Show Name, Transparent, and Single Line: Do not check these boxes.

5 Click OK to close the Text dialog box.

You can resize text boxes at any time. Ctrl-click (Windows) or Command-click (Mac) a text box. Sizing dots appear — click and drag any of them to resize the text box.

MicroWorlds EX does not care whether you use lowercase or uppercase text. For example, an object named CAT *is the same as an object named* cat*. However, many programming languages are case-sensitive.*

You can format the size, color, and font of the headline to make it look how you want inside the text box. Just click inside the text box and select Text from the toolbar. Then make changes to any of the items on the Text formatting menus. A font size of 25 works well.

WRITE A WRITENEWS PROCEDURE

There is only one procedure in our Ha Ha Headlines app, the `writenews` procedure. But this procedure does several things. Remember the game plan?

- Give instructions to the user.
- Clear out the previous headline and hide the current headline.
- Ask the user questions and place the answers — with some additional text — into the hidden headline text box.
- Show the headline and read it aloud.

When you write a new procedure, start with a `to` *command!*

Let's write that procedure! Switch to the Procedures pane, and write the `writenews` procedure as shown below:

```
to writenews
announce [TYPE IN CAPS!]
hidetext
ct
pr [HEADLINE NEWS]
pr [ ]
question [CARTOON CHARACTER?]
insert answer
question [YOUR NAME]
insert se [||AND] answer
question [LARGE NUMBER?]
insert se [||FIND] answer
question [CANDY?]
insert se [||TONS OF] answer
question [ACTION VERB (ENDING IN "ING")?]
insert se [||WHILE] answer
question [COUNTRY?]
insert se [||IN] answer
showtext
say headline
end
```

We'll talk more about this code in the "Let's Make Some News!" section.

The | symbol is a pipe. It is the upright bar on the backslash key of your keyboard. Two pipes (||) create a space in your text. You'll use these a lot when formatting text!

MAKE A WRITE THE NEWS! BUTTON

After you've written the `writenews` procedure, MicroWorlds EX now recognizes it as a new command that you can use. Follow these steps to create a button to run the procedure:

1. **On the toolbar, click the Create a Button button. Then click anywhere in the workspace.**

2. **In the Button dialog box, fill in the following fields:**

   » Label: Type **Write the News!** in the Label field to name the button.

   » Instruction: Type **writenews**, which is the procedure that will run when this button is clicked.

   » Leave everything else the same.

3. **Click OK to close the Button dialog box.**

   The Write the News! button is added to the workspace.

4. **Drag the button to the top the workspace.**

The button is too small to show all the Label text. Resize the button by Ctrl-clicking (Windows) or Command-clicking (Mac) the button to reveal sizing dots. Click and drag any of them to resize the button.

Edit the button at any time by clicking the Eye Tool button and then clicking the button.

LET'S MAKE SOME NEWS!

Time to try out your Ha Ha Headlines app. Press the Write the News! button. The `announce` command executes, giving the instructions TYPE IN CAPS! to the user.

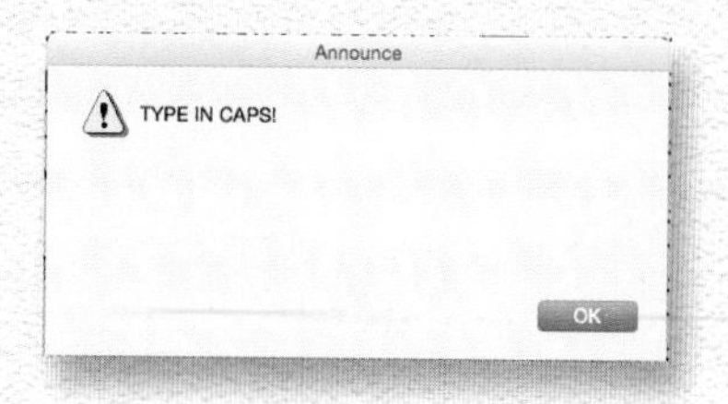

The procedure pauses until the user presses the OK button in the Announce dialog box. Then, `hidetext` hides the text box so that the user doesn't see the headline as it is being written. The next command, `ct`, clears any text that was in the text box.

Next, the first `pr` command prints the title text, HEADLINE NEWS, followed by a line break. The second `pr` command prints a blank line, followed by a line break.

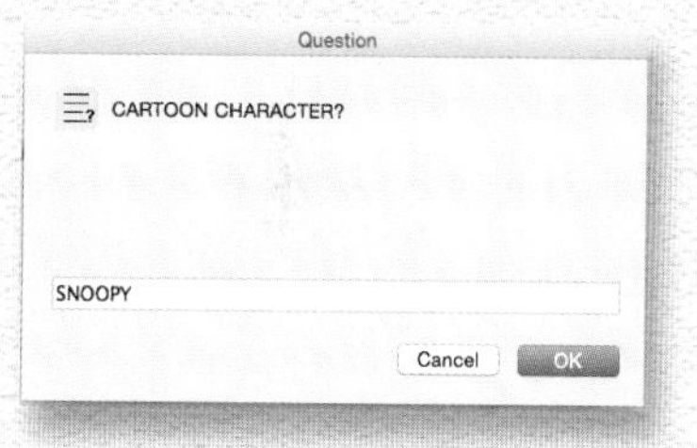

The procedure then asks the first question.

The user types in an answer and the procedure pauses until the user presses OK.

The `answer` *is a special variable. Its value is only stored until the next* `question` *is asked and a new answer value takes its place.*

As the procedure runs, it asks several questions and the user types in answers. After each question and answer, the procedure uses `insert` to join the answer with other text in brackets. All the text is added, piece by piece, to the `headline` text box until the entire headline is written.

The `insert` *command does not add line breaks. Use* `insert` *when adding one piece of text. Use* `insert se` *(insert sentence) to add two pieces of text.*

Another way to say "join" text is to say concatenate *text. This app concatenates strings of text, some of which are variable strings.*

Variables can be numerical, Boolean (true or false), or strings (text). Many languages make you declare, or specifically say, what type of variable you're using before you use it. But MicroWorlds EX doesn't!

The commands near the end of the `writenews` procedure are `showtext`, which reveals the finished headline, and `say headline`, which reads the headline aloud. As with all procedures, the final command is `end`. Here's the full code and a completed Ha Ha Headline.

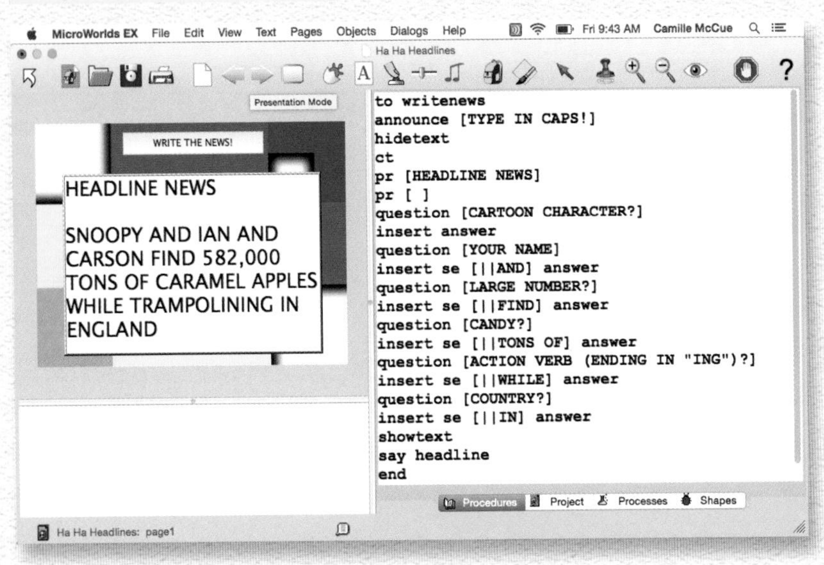

Be sure to press the Presentation Mode button on the toolbar before having a friend play with the app. You don't want the player to see the code while answering the questions!

Want to halt the app while it reads the headline to you? Just press the Stop All button on the toolbar.

ENHANCE YOUR GAME

Think of new ways to create funny news headlines or stories. You could ...

- Write a different headline in the `writenews` procedure.
- Add new pages, with each page featuring a different story.
- Change the voice that reads the story by using the `sayas` command (choose Help and then choose Vocabulary from the menu bar for details).
- Use `sayas` to read dialogue in different voices for different characters.

SAVE, TEST, AND DEBUG

Choose File and then choose Save Project from the menu bar to save your game.

Test your app by playing it repeatedly and fixing any bugs. One of the most common sources of bugs is forgetting to close square brackets in the code.

Now, see how many hilarious headlines you and your friends can make!

LAST LOOK ... BIG IDEAS IN CODING

In Ha Ha Headlines, you discovered how to handle text while making a fun app! Many of the ideas you learned here will be useful in other programming projects. Here's one last look at some of these big ideas.

BIG IDEAS IN CODING

`announce`
MAKE A TEXT ANNOUNCEMENT

`question, answer`
ASK FOR AND ACCEPT INPUT

`insert, pr, se`
`hidetext, showtext`
HANDLE AND FORMAT TEXT

`say`
PRODUCE TEXT-TO-SPEECH

USER INPUT
ASKING THE USER TO TYPE TEXT

TEXT HANDLING
PUTTING TOGETHER TEXT IN CERTAIN WAYS

STRING VARIABLES
ACCEPTING USER-INPUT TEXT AND JOINING TEXT TO MAKE NEW OUTPUT

PROGRAM OUTPUT
GIVING THE USER TEXT OR AUDIO MESSAGES

PROJECT 6 FIND FRIENDLY

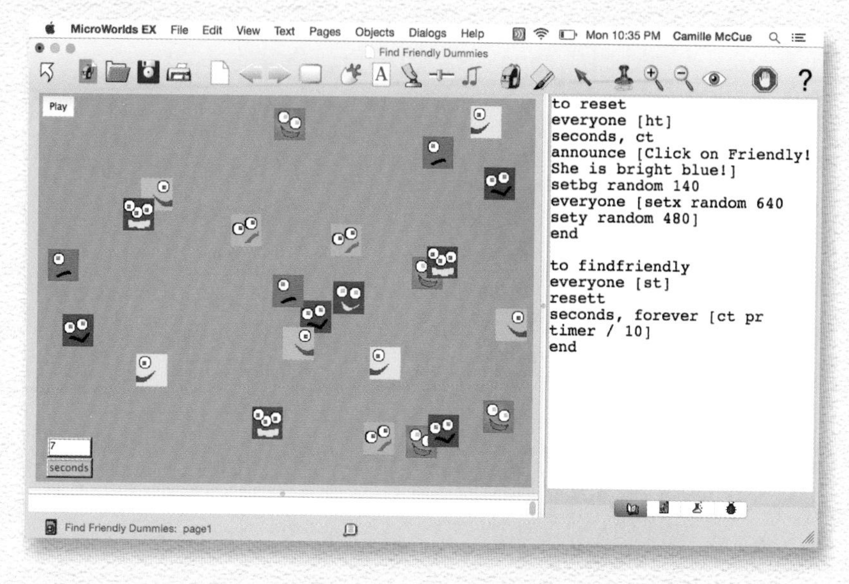

IN FIND FRIENDLY, YOU MAKE YOUR OWN SEARCH-AND-FIND PUZZLE WITH FUNNY, FOUR-SIDED FAMILY MEMBERS GETTING TOGETHER FOR A REUNION! Friendly's relatives are all sorts of fun colors, but Friendly is the only one who is bright blue! Your puzzle will challenge players to find Friendly as fast as possible!

BRAINSTORM

Use any characters and setting you want for your search-and-find! Challenge players to search for Waldo in a crowd of people or Stuart in a factory full of Minions. Your creativity is your only limit!

GAME PLAN

The game plan for building the search-and-find puzzle shows that the game needs both graphics and code. The project lets you draw lots of characters, so have fun! Remember, this is a plan for making the puzzle, not a flow chart of game operation.

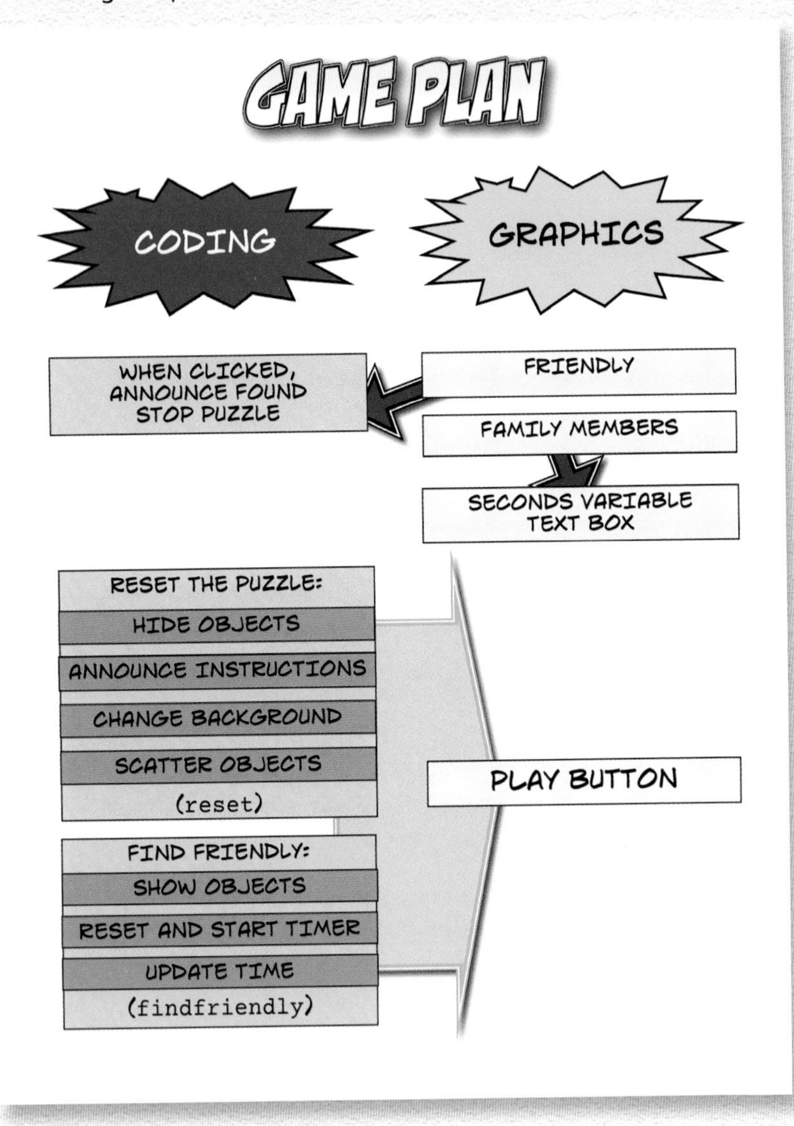

START A NEW PROJECT

Begin Find Friendly by starting a new project:

1. **Start MicroWorlds EX.**
2. **On the yellow MicroWorlds EX startup screen, select Free Mode.**

   A new project opens.
3. **Choose New Project Size from the File menu and select Full Screen 640 x 480.**

   The workspace appears.

ADD FRIENDLY

The puzzle has many turtle objects. The player looks for the object wearing the Friendly shape, so create her first.

1. **On the toolbar, click the Create a Turtle button. Move into the workspace and click to hatch a turtle.**

   Notice that when we point to this turtle, its name, `t1`, shows. You will get rid of this a little later — you don't want any names showing when you point to objects in a search-and-find!

2. **On the project's Shapes pane, double-click a shape spot.**

   The Shape Editor opens.
3. **Use the painting tools in the Shape Editor to paint Friendly.**

   Give her at least one special feature to make her different from everyone else, such as a blue color.

Note that you don't have to name this shape, but you can if you want to do so. If you don't name it, it will be known as shape 1.

4 **Press OK.**

The Friendly shape appears in a shape spot in the Shapes.

5 **Move into the workspace and click the turtle.**

The turtle now wears the Friendly shape.

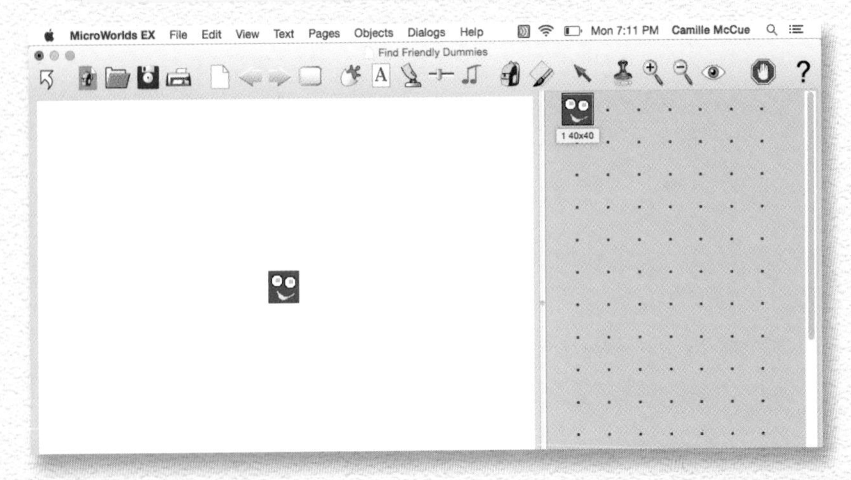

An easy way to make eyes is using the Pencil tool and the medium circle brush with an edge. Set the color to white and then click once in the Shape Editor workspace to leave an eyeball shape.

If you accidentally click somewhere other than the turtle, the Friendly shape will appear on the background — just right-click (Windows) or Control-click (Mac) the shape and select Remove from the pop-up menu to get rid of it.

KNOW WHEN FRIENDLY IS FOUND

There are many turtle objects in this puzzle, but only one needs to know if she is found. Friendly needs to know what to do when the player clicks on her!

1. **On the toolbar, click the Eye Tool button and then click the turtle wearing the Friendly shape.**

   The turtle backpack opens.

2. **At the Rules tab, type** announce [You found me!] stopall **in the OnClick field. Leave the radio button set to Once.**

3. **These instructions run one time when a player finds Friendly and clicks on her! The `stopall` instruction stops a timer that you will add later.**

4. **Close the backpack.**

ADD FAMILY MEMBERS

Add other characters who get in the way of finding Friendly. These are called *distractor* characters because they *distract* the player. Just follow the steps in the "Add Friendly" section to create new shapes, and then put them on new turtle objects. Fill your workspace with all sorts of crazy distractor characters!

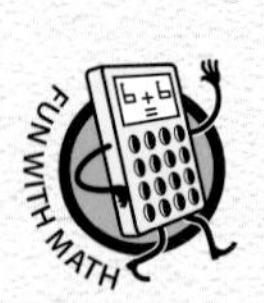

All these little squares hanging out together may remind you of a math story called, "Flatland," written by Edwin Abbott in 1884. Many students have learned about the 2D plane and 3D space by reading about Flatlanders — including a guy named A Square. An animated movie was also made about Flatland. Check it out!

ADD A TIMER

The puzzle needs a way to keep track of how many seconds it takes a player to find Friendly. Make a text box to show the number of seconds counted by the timer.

1 From the toolbar, click the Create a Text Box button; move into the workspace and drag out a little rectangle for the timer.

2 Click the Eye Tool on the Toolbar, then click the text box. Fill in this information in the Text dialog box that appears.

- Name: Type **seconds**.
- Show Name, Visible, Single Line: Check these boxes.
- Transparent: Do not check this box. Text boxes that show variables (like a timer counting seconds) must be opaque.

3 Click OK.

The text box label now shows *seconds*. Note: The text box is not a timer, but it will show the timer counting when your puzzle is finished.

4 Drag the little text box to the corner of the workspace. You don't want it to get in the way of the search-and-find puzzle.

To resize a text box, Ctrl-click (Windows) or Command-click (Mac) the button and pull on the sizing dots.

If you need to edit the text box, click the Eye Tool on the toolbar and then click the text box.

WRITE A RESET PROCEDURE

Your game will use a `reset` procedure to reset the puzzle for the player.

On the project's Procedures pane, write the `reset` procedure:

```
to reset
everyone [ht]
seconds, ct
announce [Click on Friendly! She is bright blue!]
setbg random 140
everyone [setx random 640
sety random 480]
end

to findfriendly
everyone [st]
resett
seconds, forever [ct pr timer / 10]
end
```

Procedures | Project | Processes | Shapes

Here's what the `reset` procedure does:

The `everyone [ht]` command hides all the characters. Then, `seconds, ct` clears text from the seconds variable text box. The `announce` command gives the player directions for playing.

The last two commands add some randomness to the puzzle. The `setbg random 140` command sets the background to a random color. Finally, the `everyone [setx random 640 sety random 480]` command scatters the turtle objects into random positions all over the workspace.

Previously, you set background colors by naming them with a command such as `setbg "orange`. *Colors can also be set by number with a command such as* `setbg 25`. *The* `random 140` *code produces a random number from 0 to 139.*

Apps often need objects put into random places. The position of a turtle object is its coordinates. The x-coordinate tells where the turtle is positioned left to right in the workspace. The y-coordinate tells where the turtle is bottom to top.

In the Find Friendly puzzle, the workspace is 640 pixels wide. So, `setx random 640` gives the turtle a random number for its x-coordinate. Also, the workspace is 480 pixels high. So, `sety random 480` gives the turtle a random number for its y-coordinate. Giving every object in the puzzle random numbers for its coordinates ends up scattering the objects all over the workspace.

When typing procedures in the Procedures pane, sometimes a really long command wraps onto the next line. This is not a problem! But don't add a line break at the wrap point — this will create a problem.

WRITE A FINDFRIENDLY PROCEDURE

Your puzzle will use a `findfriendly` procedure to start the search-and-find action.

On the project's Procedures pane, add the `findfriendly` procedure shown in the previous figure.

Here's what the `findfriendly` procedure does:

The `everyone [st]` command shows all the characters. Then, `resett` resets the timer to 0 and starts counting! variable text box. The command `seconds, forever [ct pr timer / 10]` shows the number of seconds that have passed in the text box named `seconds`. The `forever` command runs the commands in the brackets over and over in an infinite loop. Those commands are `ct` (clear text), `pr` (print), and `timer / 10`. This shows a running clock of how many seconds it takes the player to find Friendly.

The timer counts in tenths of a second. When one second has passed, it shows the number 10. To show the real number of seconds, you have to take the number on the timer and divide by 10: `timer / 10`.

MAKE A PLAY BUTTON

After you've written the `reset` procedure and the `findfriendly` procedure, MicroWorlds EX recognizes them as commands that you can use. Follow these steps to create a button to run the procedures:

1. **On the toolbar, click the Create a Button button, and then click anywhere in the workspace.**
2. **In the Button dialog box, fill in the following fields:**
   - Label: Type **Play** in the Label field to name the button.
   - Instruction: Type **reset findfriendly** in the Instruction field. This first runs the `reset` procedure, then the `findfriendly` procedure.
   - Leave everything else the same.
3. **Click OK to close the Button dialog box.**

   The Play button is added to the workspace.
4. **Drag the button to the upper-left corner of the workspace.**

This search-and-find puzzle is an abstraction of searching and finding in the real world. In computer science, you work to make abstractions of more complicated things. An abstraction is a simpler version of something that only focuses on the most important parts of the thing so that you don't have to worry about too many details.

Find Friendly always has the same objects in the same population and only one Friendly. This is easier than building a puzzle that has changing objects, or different numbers of objects. But you could add these new features later, to better match the real-world searching and finding — like police detective work!

FINAL TOUCHES

You need two final touches to finish your puzzle:

- Remove the tool tips. In the Command Center, type **everyone [settooltip "]** and press Enter (Windows) or Return (Mac). Now, when a player points at a character, it won't show the name of the turtle object anymore!
- Bring Friendly to the front. Right-click (Windows) or Control-click (Mac) on Friendly and select Bring to Front from the pop-up menu. This will make sure that Friendly can't hide behind another character, making it impossible to find her.
- And, you're done! Find Friendly looks similar to this:

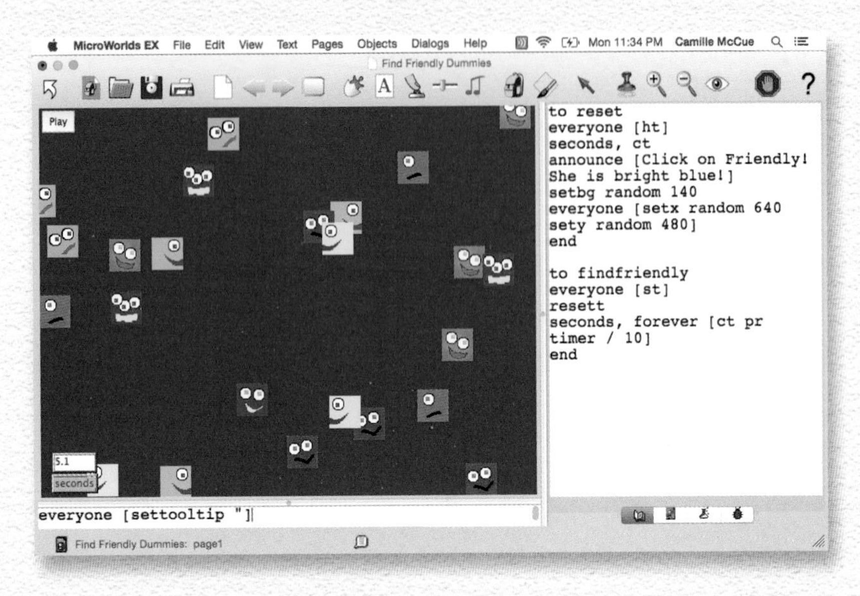

Press the Presentation Mode button on the toolbar before having a friend try the search-and-find.

ENHANCE YOUR GAME

Now that you are finished creating your puzzle, why not add new features to it? Add new shapes. Or animate every character so that all the objects move around, making it more difficult to find Friendly (don't forget to add an `everyone [clickon]` command into the `findfriendly` procedure to get all the objects moving). Or make all the objects very small and double or triple the number of objects to really make the puzzle challenging!

SAVE, TEST, AND DEBUG

Choose File and then chose Save Project from the menu bar to save your puzzle.

Test your project by playing it repeatedly. When players press the Play button, they see this:

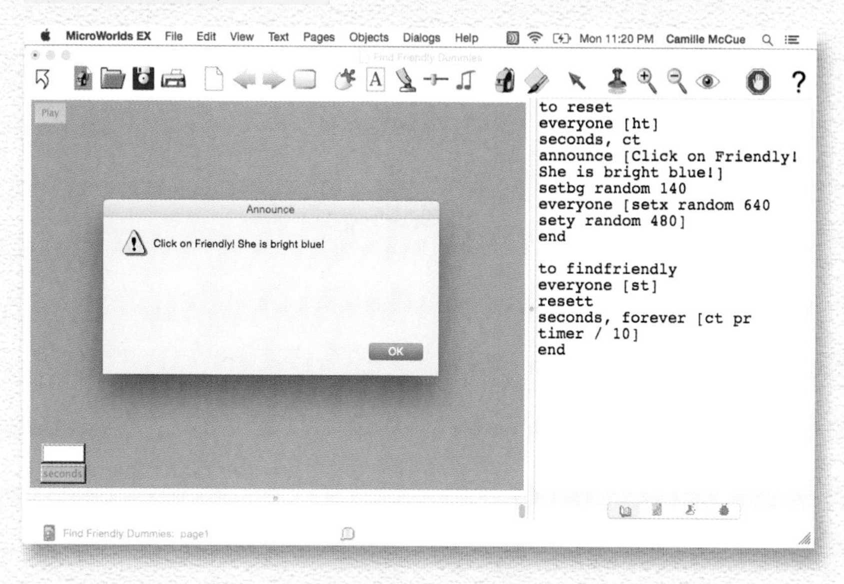

A player who successfully finds Friendly sees this message:

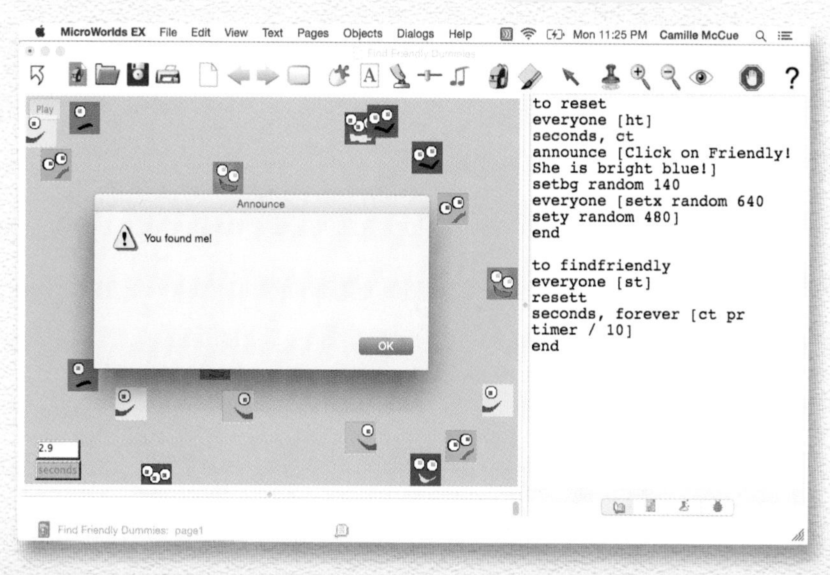

After you have worked out all the bugs, challenge friends and family to see who is the fastest at Find Friendly!

LAST LOOK ... BIG IDEAS IN CODING

In Find Friendly, you made your own search-and-find puzzle. Many of the ideas you discovered here will be used in other programming projects. Here's a final look at some of these big ideas.

BIG IDEAS IN CODING

`random`
MAKE A RANDOM NUMBER

`onclick`
DO SOMETHING WHEN AN OBJECT IS CLICKED ON

`ht, st`
HIDE TURTLE OBJECT, SHOW TURTLE OBJECT

`timer, resett`
USE TIMER, RESET TIMER

`stopall`
STOP PROGRAM EXECUTION

SCATTER OBJECTS
SET OBJECT COORDINATES TO RANDOM POSITIONS.

HIDE / SHOW OBJECTS
KEEP OBJECTS SECRET OR REVEAL THEM.

INTERACT WITH OBJECT
MOUSE CLICK AN OBJECT TO MAKE SOMETHING HAPPEN.

TIMERS
RESET A TIMER, SHOW HOW MUCH TIME HAS PASSED, OR STOP A TIMER.

PROJECT 7 HUNGRY BOBO

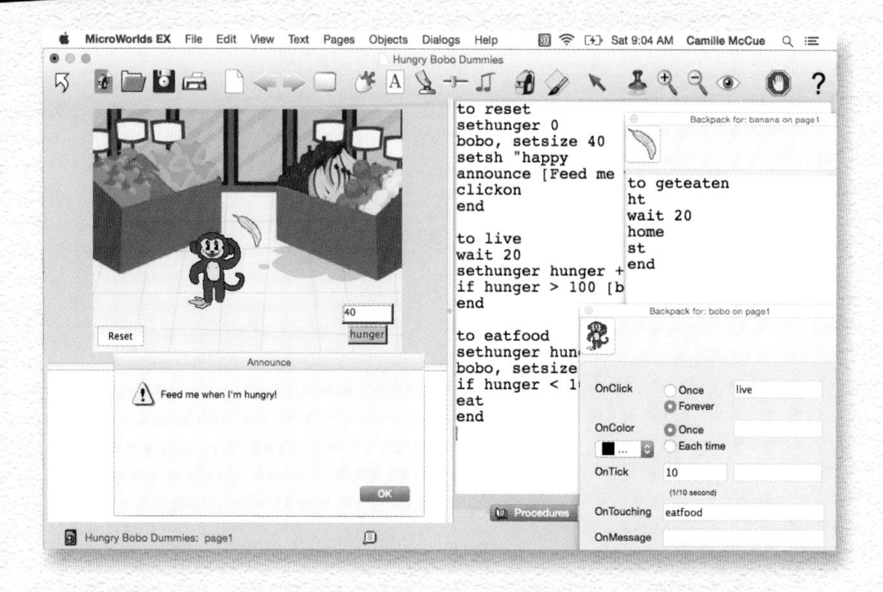

IN THIS PROJECT, YOU CREATE A VIRTUAL PET NAMED BOBO THE MONKEY. Bobo is a type of toy called a Tamagotchi pet that has been popular in Japan. Changing shapes and a variable show Bobo's emotions and hunger level. Although he doesn't eat real food, Bobo is a hungry little guy, so users playing with your Bobo toy will need to feed him digital bananas — a lot of them — to keep him happy!

BRAINSTORM

I've had students make all sorts of crazy Tama pets. There have been Tamas named Tinky, BanMan, Bunny, and Fluffo Sheep. One student made a greedy Alien Tama, and another made a World War II Solider Tama!

Use your imagination to invent a character you like, as well as variables that show the health and happiness of your "pet" as it lives on your computer.

GAME PLAN

Here's a game plan for building your Hungry Bobo toy. You will create simple graphics and write code. Keep this plan in mind as you work through the steps.

GAME PLAN

GRAPHICS & SOUND

BACKGROUND

LIVE:

HUNGER RISES WITH TIME

IF HUNGER HIGH, PET SAD

(live)

PET OBJECT

happy AND sad SHAPES

EAT SOUND

EAT FOOD:

PLAY EAT SOUND

REDUCE HUNGER

GROW PET

IF HUNGER LOW, PET HAPPY

(eatfood)

GET EATEN

FOOD OBJECT

HUNGER METER

RESET THE PET

RESET BUTTON

START A NEW PROJECT

Begin Hungry Bobo by starting a new project:

1. **Start MicroWorlds EX.**
2. **On the yellow MicroWorlds EX startup screen, select Free Mode.**

   A new project opens.

3. **From the menu bar, choose File and then choose New Project Size and select any project size you want.**

APPLY A BACKGROUND

Bobo can live anywhere, but since he's hungry, let's put him near a fruit and vegetable stand so he can easily grab a banana!

1. **From the toolbar, click the Hide/Show Painting/Clipart button.**

   The Painting/Clipart palette opens.

2. **Click the Backgrounds button to show the available backgrounds you can choose.**

3. **Click the grocery background, and then click in the workspace to apply the background image.**
4. **Right-click (Windows) or Control-click (Mac) the background image. From the pop-up menu, select Stamp Full Page.**

   The image fills the entire workspace.

5. **Leave the Painting/Clipart palette open — you'll need it in the next steps.**

ADD BOBO

The toy has two turtle objects. One of these wears monkey shapes, so create it first.

1 On the toolbar, click the Create a Turtle button. Move into the workspace and click to hatch a turtle.

Drag it to a position on the floor in front of the produce stands.

2 In the Painting/Clipart palette, click the Singles.

3 Scroll to find the monkey shape.

4 Click the monkey shape and drag it to a shape spot. Repeat.

There are now two monkey shapes in the Shapes pane.

5 On the Shapes pane, double-click one of the monkey shapes.

The Shape Editor opens.

6 Use the drawing tools in the Shape Editor to make the monkey look happy. Put a smile on his face and a gleam in his eyes!

7 Name the shape `happy` (in the empty white field at the top of the Shape Editor) and then click OK.

The Shape Editor closes, and the `happy` shape appears in the Shapes pane.

8 Repeat Steps 5 and 6 on the other monkey to create a sad shape. Make the monkey mouth frown. Use the eraser tool in the Painting/Clipart palette to take away the banana. Also, erase the tail and redraw it so that it is pointing down.

9 Name the edited monkey shape `sad` (in the empty white field at the top of the Shape Editor) and then click OK.

The Shape Editor closes, and the `sad` shape appears in the Shapes pane.

10 Click either one of the shapes, `happy` or `sad`, and then move into the workspace and click the turtle.

The turtle object now wears the shape.

If you accidentally click somewhere other than the turtle, the monkey shape will appear on the background — just right-click (Windows) or Control-click (Mac) the shape and select Remove from the pop-up menu to get rid of it.

NAME BOBO

Turtle objects in this project will be named. Bobo needs a name because it needs to know when you are giving commands only to it.

1 On the toolbar, click the Eye Tool button and then click the turtle wearing the monkey shape.

The turtle backpack opens.

Remember that the turtle backpack holds all the turtle's important directions. This project uses the State tab, which had information. It also uses the Procedures tab and the Rules tab (which has instructions for the turtle to follow).

2 At the State tab, click the Edit button next to the Name field.

3 In the Name dialog box that appears, type bobo **in the Name field.**

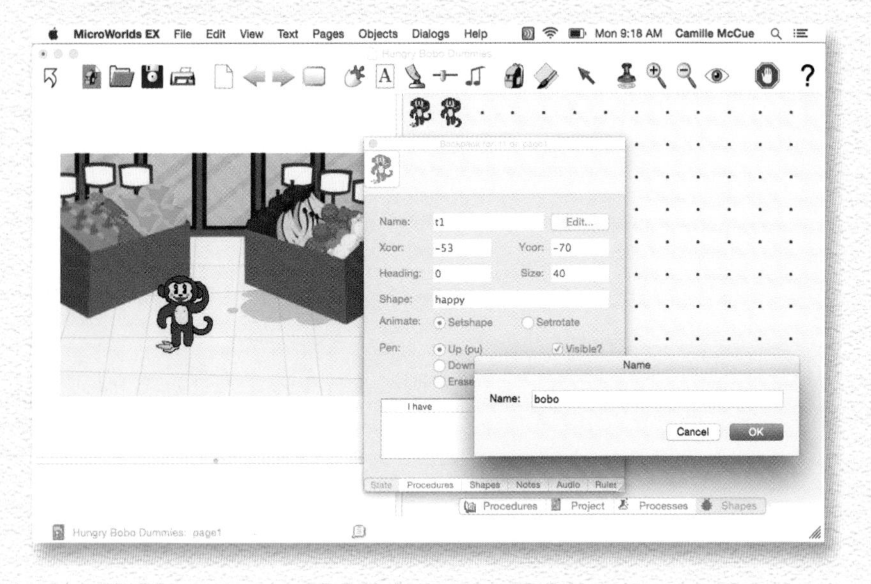

4. **Click OK to close the Name dialog box.**
5. **Close Bobo's backpack for now.**

ADD A SOUND

When Bobo eats a banana, the user hears an eating sound. Add the sound as follows:

1. **At the menu bar, choose File, choose Import, and then choose Import Sound.**

   The Import Sound dialog box opens.

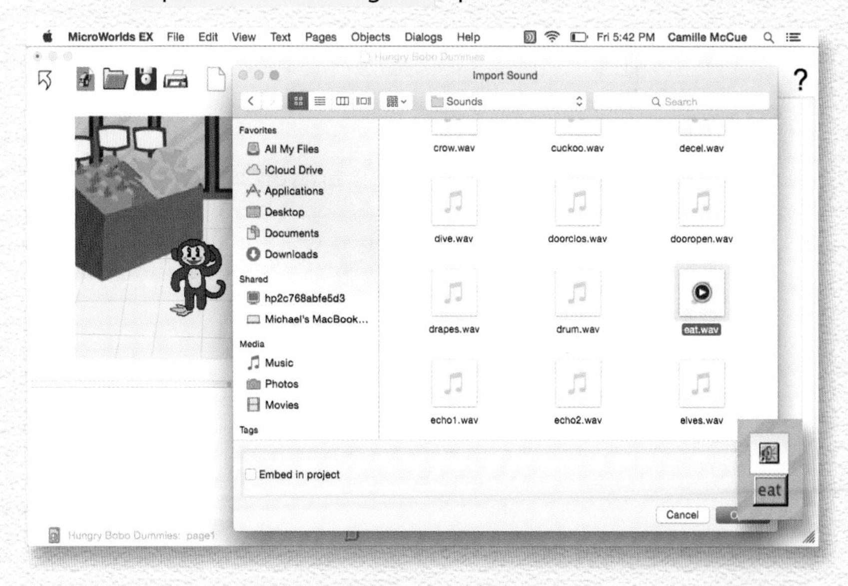

2. **Navigate to the MicroWorlds EX folder, then the Sound folder.**

   You may have to use the Search box to find the MicroWorlds EX folder.

3. **Select the eat.wav sound and then press the Open button.**

The sound is added to your project. The `eat` sound icon appears in the workspace. Press the icon to play the sound! Later, you will make this sound play when Bobo eats his banana.

4 Hide the `eat` sound icon so that users don't see it onscreen. Click the Eye Tool button and then click the sound icon.

The Media dialog box appears.

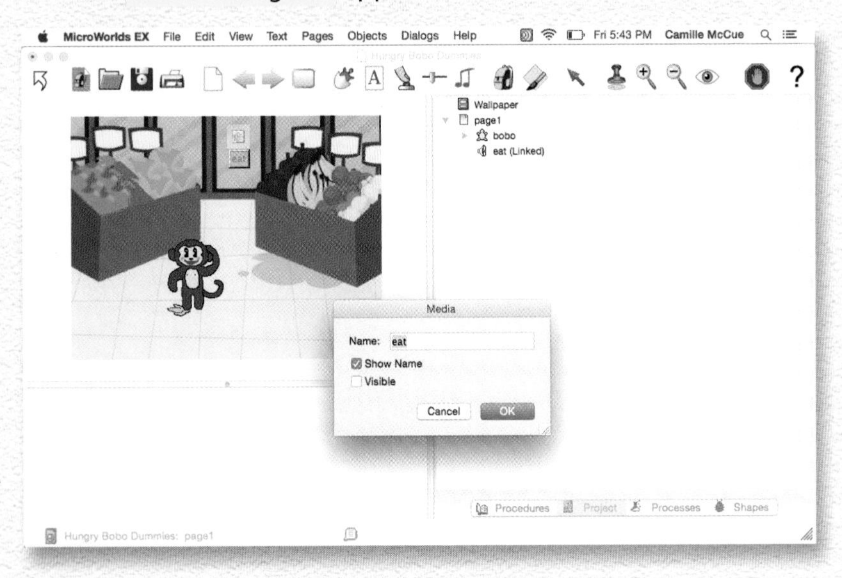

5 In the Media dialog box, uncheck the Visible box. Click OK.

The `eat` sound icon is now hidden in the workspace.

If you need to need to bring back the hidden sound icon, open the Project pane by pressing the Project tab at the bottom-right of the MicroWorlds EX interface. Press the arrow next to `page1` to show all the objects on the page. Then right-click (Windows) or Control-click (Mac) the sound name and select Show from the pop-up menu.

ADD A BANANA

The second turtle object is a banana.

1 **On the toolbar, click the Create a Turtle button. Move into the workspace and click to hatch a turtle.**

Drag it to the middle of the workspace.

2 **On the Shapes pane, double-click a shape spot.**

The Shape Editor opens.

3 **Use the drawing tools in the Shape Editor to draw a banana shape.**

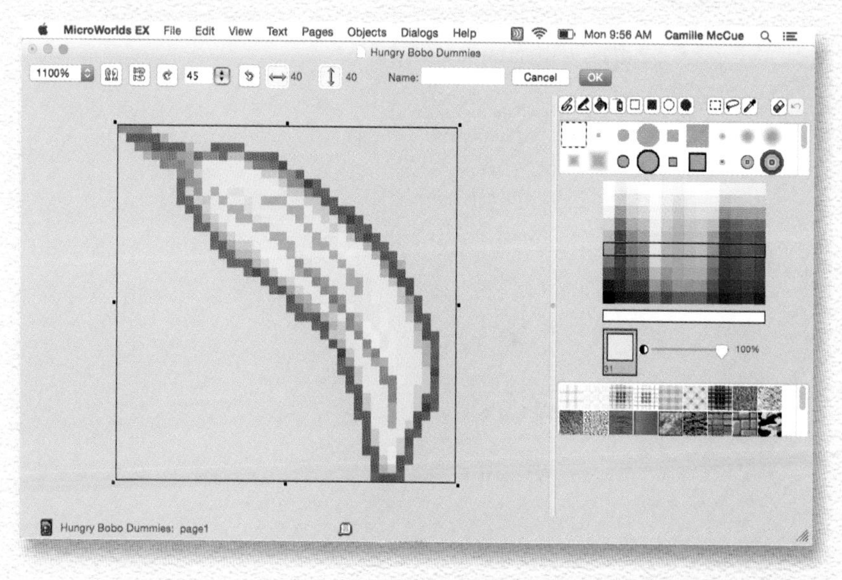

You don't need to name this shape — we will name *the turtle* wearing this shape in the next section.

4 **Click OK to close the Shape Editor.**

The shape appears in the Shapes pane.

5 **Click the turtle object you created in Step 1.**

The turtle object now wears the shape.

NAME THE BANANA

The banana object needs a name because it needs to know when you are giving commands only to it.

1. **On the toolbar, click the Eye Tool button and then click the turtle wearing the banana shape.**

   The turtle backpack opens.

2. **At the State tab, click the Edit button next to the Name field.**

3. **In the Name dialog box that appears, type** banana **in the Name field.**

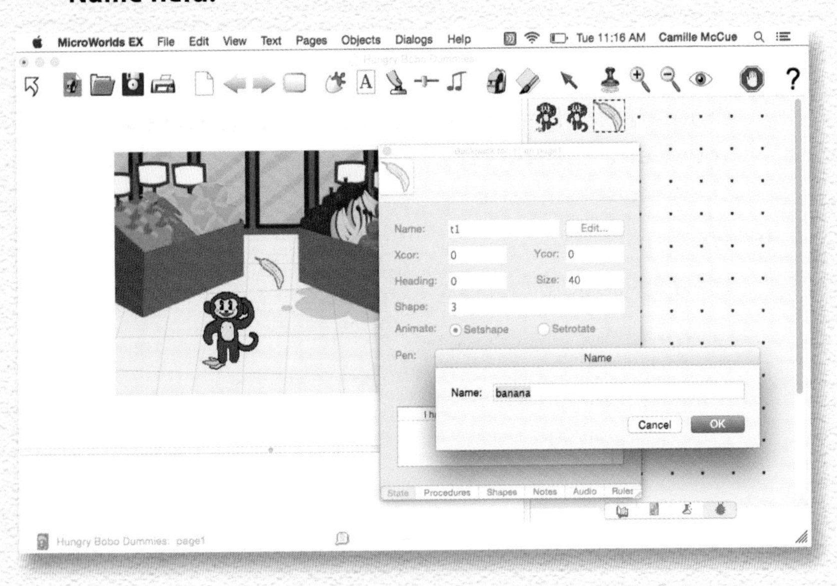

4. **Click OK to close the Name dialog box.**

5. **Close the banana's backpack for now.**

Naming things is an important job in coding. This project has names for turtle objects, shapes, and procedures. Calling things by names helps you know what you are using at different places in the code. MicroWorlds EX does not care whether names have capital or lowercase letters, but some programming languages do! Just be sure not to use spaces in coded names.

CREATE A HUNGER VARIABLE

Your app needs a way to measure how hungry Bobo is feeling! It needs a variable called *hunger*. Create a hunger variable as follows:

1. **From the toolbar, click the Create a Text Box button; move into the workspace and drag out a rectangle for the text box.**
2. **In the Text box dialog box, fill in the following information:**
   - Name: Type **hunger**.
   - Show Name and Visible: Check these boxes.
   - Leave everything else unchecked.
3. **Click OK.**

   The text box label now shows *hunger*.
4. **Drag the text box to anywhere you want.**
5. **If you need to edit the text box, click the Eye Tool on the toolbar and then click the text box.**

Once your pet is completed, this variable text box will serve as a “hunger meter” to show users how hungry Bobo is feeling!

WRITE A RESET PROCEDURE

The `reset` procedure resets the app so that Bobo is "starting out fresh."

Switch to the Procedures pane, and write the `reset` procedure as shown below:

```
to reset
sethunger 0
bobo, setsize 40
setsh "happy
announce [Feed me when I'm hungry!]
clickon
end
```

Like all procedures, `reset` starts with the word `to`, followed by the name of the procedure. Then `sethunger 0` resets the hunger variable so that your pet is not hungry at all. The command `bobo, setsize 40` talks only to the monkey and tells it to set its size to 40.

Because we are already talking to `bobo`, the next command of `setsh "happy` is executed only by him. This sets his starting shape to a happy one because he isn't hungry!

Next, he announces that the user should feed him when he is hungry. When the active object (`bobo`) is "clicked on," the code in the OnClick field of his backpack runs. You will add that code shortly. As with all procedures, the final command is `end`.

All computer code relies on three structures: sequential execution, branching, *and* looping. *The* `reset` *code is sequential because it simply runs one step, then the next step, in order until it reaches the end.*

MAKE A RESET BUTTON

After you've written the `reset` procedure, MicroWorlds EX now recognizes it as a new command that you can use. Follow these steps to create a button to run the procedure:

1. **On the toolbar, click the Create a Button button. Then click anywhere in the workspace.**
2. **In the Button dialog box, fill in the following fields:**

   » Label: Type **Reset** in the Label field to name the button.

   » Instruction: Type **reset**, which is the procedure that will run when this button is clicked.

   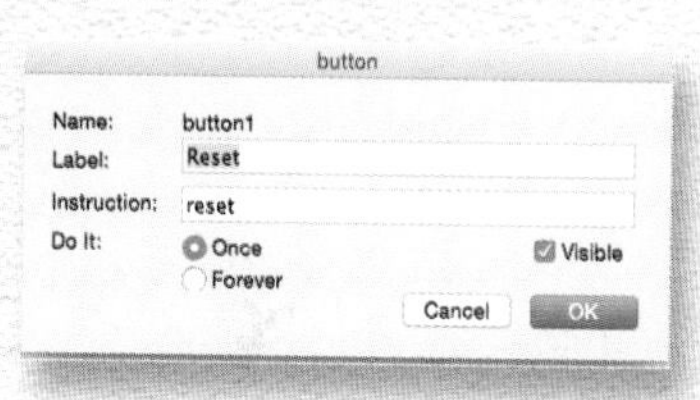

   » Leave everything else the same.

3. **Click OK to close the Button dialog box.**

   The Reset button is added to the workspace.

4. **Drag the button to wherever you want in the workspace.**
5. **Edit a button at any time by clicking the Eye Tool button and then clicking the button.**

WRITE A LIVE PROCEDURE

The `live` procedure makes Bobo hungrier as time goes by.

At the Procedures pane, write the `live` procedure as shown below:

```
to live
wait 20
sethunger hunger + 20
if hunger > 100 [bobo, setsh "sad]
end
```

This procedure starts with `to` followed by the procedure name, `live`. The `wait 20` is a two-second pause. This lets Bobo's hunger rise slowly over time. Then, `sethunger hunger + 20` increases the `hunger` variable by 20. Finally, the `if hunger > 100 [bobo, setsh "sad]` is a conditional statement: When the `hunger` value rises to a value greater than 100, the `bobo` object sets it shape to `sad`. The procedure ends with `end`.

ADD LIVE TO BOBO'S BACKPACK

Remember that the `reset` procedure has a command to `clickon` Bobo. When Bobo is "clicked on," he will do something. The something you want him to do is live! Here's how to code this:

1. **On the toolbar, click the Eye Tool button and then click Bobo.**

   The turtle backpack opens.

2. **At the Rules tab, type** live **in the OnClick field.**

3. **Set the OnClick radio button to Forever.**

4. **Leave Bobo's backpack open.**

Now, when `clickon` executes, it runs `live` forever in an endless loop.

The live code runs in a forever loop because there is no code to "break out of it." It will execute until you click Bobo again to "click off" the monkey or press the Stop All button.

WRITE AN EATFOOD PROCEDURE

The `eatfood` procedure lets Bobo eat.

At the Procedures pane, write the `eatfood` procedure as shown below:

```
to eatfood
sethunger hunger - 50
bobo, setsize size + 2
if hunger < 100 [bobo, setsh "happy]
eat
end
```

This procedure starts with `to` followed by the procedure name. The `sethunger hunger - 50` command decreases the `hunger` variable by 50. Then, `bobo, setsize size + 2` grows the monkey because he's eating. (You have to talk just to Bobo to make sure that only Bobo grows, not the banana!)

Next, the `if hunger < 100 [bobo, setsh "happy]` is a conditional statement: When the `hunger` value drops to a value less than 100, the `bobo` object sets it shape to `happy` because his hunger is low. Lastly, the procedure plays the `eat` sound you imported earlier. (If you did not import a sound, leave out this command.) The procedure ends with `end`.

The `live` *and* `eatfood` *procedures contain conditional codes. A conditional can branch out of a procedure to run code that is not sequential (such as changing the object's shape) and then return to the procedure where it left off.*

ADD EATFOOD TO BOBO'S BACKPACK

When Bobo is touched by an object, he eats it! Here's how to code this:

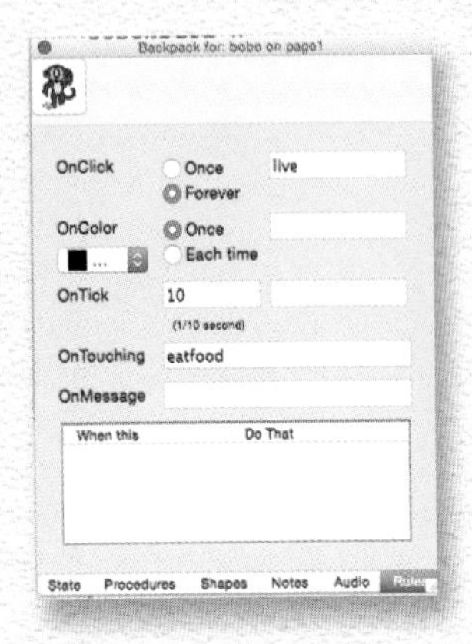

1. **Bobo's backpack should already be open. If it isn't, click the Eye Tool button and then click Bobo to open the backpack.**
2. **At the Rules tab, type** eatfood **in the OnTouching field.**
3. **Close Bobo's backpack.**

Now, when an object touches Bobo, the `eatfood` procedure executes.

The `live` *procedure is running in a forever loop, and the* `eatfood` *procedure runs if Bobo is touched. So more than one procedure can run at the same time in your program — this is called* parallel execution.

WRITE AND ADD A GETEATEN PROCEDURE

Because there are only two objects in this program, the only object that can touch Bobo is the banana. A user feeds Bobo by dragging the banana to him. When this happens, the two objects touch. The banana should disappear as though it has been eaten. Then, after a brief pause, the banana should reappear so that Bobo can eat again later.

All the procedures you have written so far have been in the project Procedures pane. These are *global* procedures. This means that every element in the project (objects, variables, and other elements if they existed) can use the procedures.

For the banana, you will write a `geteaten` procedure to show and hide the banana. Since only the banana needs to know this procedure, you write it inside the banana object. This is a *local* procedure. A local procedure can only be run by the object that contains it.

Write the `geteaten` procedure inside the banana as follows:

1. **At the Toolbar, click the Eye Tool button and then click the banana to open its backpack.**
2. **At the Procedures tab (see below left), type the `geteaten` procedure.**
3. **At the Rules tab (see below right), type** geteaten **in the OnTouching field.**

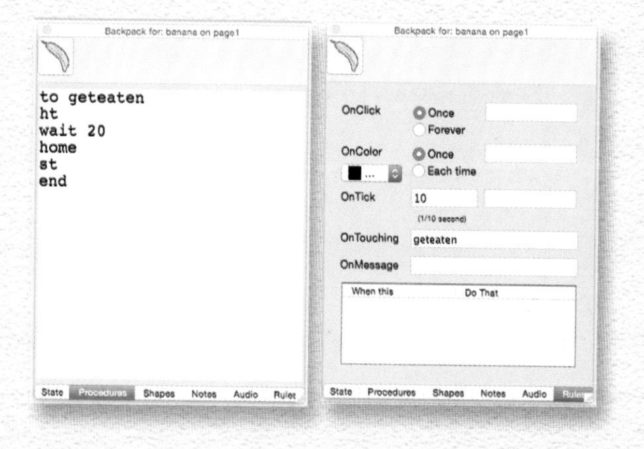

When the banana touches Bobo, the `geteaten` procedure executes. You can see that the procedure makes the banana hide, `ht`, for two seconds `wait 20`. Then the banana is moved back to `home`, at the center of the workspace, so that it is not touching the Bobo — otherwise it would be eaten again! Finally, the banana reappears with the show turtle, `st`, command.

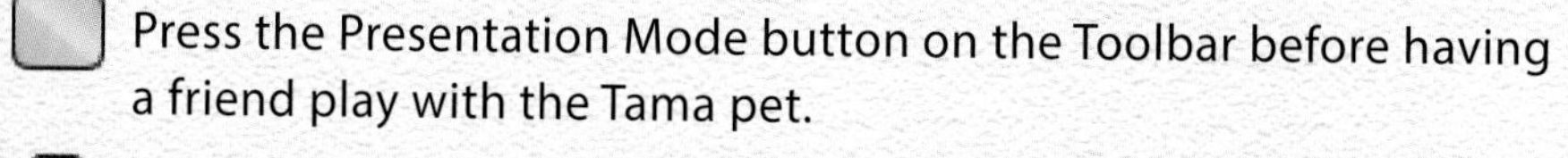

Press the Presentation Mode button on the Toolbar before having a friend play with the Tama pet.

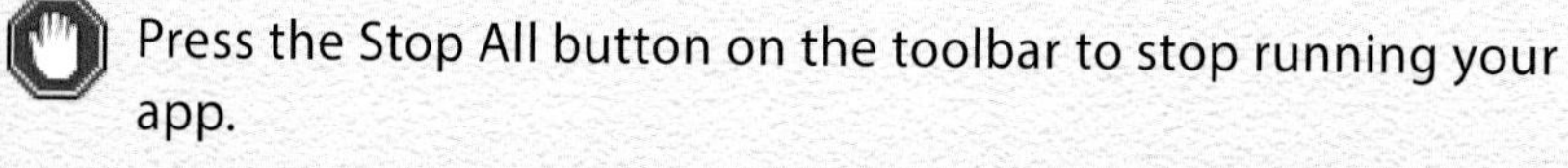

Press the Stop All button on the toolbar to stop running your app.

SAVE, TEST, AND DEBUG

Choose File and then choose Save Project from the menu bar to save your Tama pet.

Invite friends to play with your Tama. All they need to do is press the Reset button to start the app. As time passes, Bobo's hunger will rise until he looks sad. But, if the user drags a banana to Bobo for him to eat, his hunger will decrease. If his hunger is low, then he looks happy. Test the app by playing with it repeatedly and fixing any bugs.

ENHANCE YOUR GAME

Think of new ways to make your Tama pet even more interesting. You could…

- Write new conditional statements so that your pet says different things at varying hunger levels.
- Add a second variable, such as `health` or `wealth`. Write additional code to make these variables change over time.
- Add new shapes such as `starving` or `sleepy`.
- Add a melody of your own creation to the `reset` procedure. Just press the Create a Melody button on the toolbar, then make a song using the instruments and the keyboard in the dialog box. Then add the name of the tune (for example, `melody1`) to your `reset` procedure. Your original music creation will play when you press the Reset button!

LAST LOOK ... BIG IDEAS IN CODING

In Hungry Bobo, you discovered how to put together many of the ideas learned in this book to create a fun Tama pet! Here's a final look at some of these big ideas.

BIG IDEAS IN CODING

`setvariable variable + 1`
INCREASE A VARIABLE BY 1 (USING A −1 DECREASES THE VARIABLE)

`OnTouching`
WHEN OBJECTS TOUCH, RUN CODE

`if-then conditional`
IF CONDITION IS TRUE, THEN RUN THE CONSEQUENCE

`soundname`
PLAYS A SOUND WHEN THE NAME IS CALLED IN THE CODE

CONCEPTS

CONDITIONALS
CONDITIONALS CHANGE THE FLOW OF CODE EXECUTION BASED ON CERTAIN CONDITIONS.

LOCAL & GLOBAL PROCEDURES
A LOCAL PROCEDURE CAN BE RUN ONLY BY ITS OBJECT. A GLOBAL PROCEDURE CAN BE RUN BY ALL.

PARALLEL EXECUTION
RUN TWO OR MORE PROCEDURES AT THE SAME TIME.

MEDIA CALL
PLAY A SOUND OR RUN OTHER MEDIA IN YOUR PROGRAM.

AUTHOR NOTES

HOW TO CREATE A GAME PLAN WHEN WRITING A MICROWORLDS EX COMPUTER PROGRAM

Writing a new computer program begins with creating a game plan. The plan tells what smaller parts you need to make and put together to build the entire program. Your plan should contain graphics and coding parts. Start with the big picture and fill in details as you plan.

PLAN YOUR DESIGN AND GRAPHICS

1. **Define the program purpose: game, toy, simulation, or animated scene.**
2. **Select or paint a background on the page.**
3. **Create characters if needed by making turtle objects. Then select shapes from the Painting/Clipart palette, or paint new shapes in shape spots on the Shapes pane. (Double-click a shape spot to open the Shape Editor.)**
4. **Make text boxes with titles, labels, and instructions.**
5. **Make text boxes to show variable values.**

CREATE CHARACTER ACTIONS

1. **In each turtle backpack on the State tab, set character attributes.**

   This is useful for attributes that don't change during the program because after these are assigned, you don't have to set these values again. Examples include size and heading.

These values can still be changed at any time during program execution, if needed.

2. **In each turtle backpack on the Rules tab, add primitives or procedures that will execute under certain circumstances.**

   For example, a command in the OnClick field executes when the turtle is "clicked on." And a command in the OnTouching field executes when the turtle touches another turtle object.

3. **If needed, add universal color under conditionals to the background.**

   Commands added to the background will be executed when a turtle touches a chosen color.

4. **Add features, such as ways for users to interact and multimedia.**

5. **Add buttons to the graphical user interface so that users can execute the code you have written and interact with your program.**

6. **If needed, add audio features, such as music or sound effects.**

CODE THE ACTIONS

1. **In the Procedures pane, write procedures that will be executed to control program flow, react to program conditions, and react to user input.**

2. **You can also add an object-specific procedure to any turtle object by writing the procedure into the turtle backpack at the Procedures tab.**

3. **In the Procedures pane, write a reset procedure to set starting conditions for program execution.**

   This may include setting initial variable values and turtle sizes, shapes, headings, and positions, whether turtles show or hide, and whether turtles are clicked on or clicked off.

HOW TO PUBLISH YOUR MICROWORLDS EX APPS ON THE WEB

If you want to share your completed MicroWorlds EX projects with your friends or other people online — even if they don't have the MicroWorlds EX software — you can put your creations on the web. Users will see your projects in Presentation mode, but they won't be able to see or edit your project code.

To share your project via the web, you need to output your already saved project as HTML, and then upload your project to a website. In order to see a project posted on the web, users need to install the MicroWorlds plug-in. The following sections explain the steps in more detail.

OUTPUT YOUR PROJECT IN HTML

Follow these steps to output your project in HTML:

1. **In MicroWorlds EX, open your completed and saved project.**
2. **From the menu bar, choose File and then choose Create HTML Template.**

   The Choose a Folder dialog box opens.
3. **Navigate to the folder where you want to save your project.**

   It's a good idea to create a new folder for outputting your project. The program will automatically save all the files you need — the .html file (the web page that will show your project), a new copy of the MicroWorlds EX project itself, and all the linked media.

4. **Click the Choose button.**

   All the files for your MicroWorlds EX project (for example, your .mwx file, the HTML file, and any linked media such as sounds) are saved in the same folder.

UPLOAD YOUR PROJECT TO THE WEB

To post your MicroWorlds EX project on the web, you must have access to a website hosted on a server, and upload capabilities, such as FTP file transfer. Upload the entire contents of the folder you just created (your .mwx project file, the .html web page file, and any linked files) to the server hosting your website using the procedure you typically follow.

HELP YOUR WEBSITE VISITORS INSTALL THE MICROWORLDS EX PLUG-IN

Users who visit your website require two items in order to view your project online:

- The MicroWorlds EX plug-in for their computer operating system (Windows or Mac). Users need to download and install the MicroWorlds EX plug-in only once (that is, not each time you create a new project).
- A link to the .html file that shows your project.

Windows users can view your project in the current versions of Internet Explorer, Chrome, and Firefox. Mac users can view your project in Safari, Chrome, and Firefox.

Follow these steps to provide these two items via the web:

1. **When you post your project online, you need to provide a link for users to download a MicroWorlds EX plug-in for Windows and for Mac. Go to MicroWorlds (www.microworlds.com) and look for the Mac and Windows plug-ins on the home page.**

2. **Post the following instructions on your web page so that users know what to do with the Windows and Mac plug-ins:**

   » **Window instructions:** First, download the MicroWorldsPlugin.exe file. Next, close any browser that is open. After the file is downloaded, double-click to launch it. The installation process will start. Follow the instructions. Relaunch your browser.

   » **Mac instructions:** First, download the MicroWorldsPlugin.zip file. Next, close any browser that is open. After it's downloaded, extract (unzip) the files inside the .zip file (if they do not do so automatically). Look for the unzipped file in your Downloads folder. Double-click the file and follow the instructions for installation. Relaunch your browser.

3. **Post a link to the .html file containing your MicroWorlds EX project. Using your website editing software, create a hyperlink to the URL of the .html web page of your project.**

GLOSSARY

abstraction In computer science, you work to make abstractions of more complicated things. An abstraction is a simpler version of something that only focuses on the most important parts of the thing so that you don't have to worry about too many details. The board game Operation and the digital game Operations are both abstractions of a real surgical operation.

app An application. The result of combining computer code and graphics to create a finished program that people can use.

backpack A turtle backpack is like your backpack. It contains all the turtle's important information and rules. There are tabs at the bottom of the backpack window that organize the backpack into sections.

collision A collision occurs when two objects have coordinate convergence – parts that occupy the same coordinates. This happens when two objects hit each other.

concatenate Join together. Usually applies to strings of text and variable values.

conditional A logic statement that is common in coding. Conditionals allow to the program to branch to different parts of the program. If-then conditionals are one of the most basic types of conditionals. The general form is if condition then consequence.

coordinate A number that gives the x-position or the y-position of an object. Coordinates are integers (positive, zero, or negative numbers).

debug Remove the errors (bugs) from your computer program to make it execute the way you want.

default A starting value or attribute, assigned to an element when you first create the element. For example, the starting size of a turtle object in MicroWorlds EX is 40.

efficient Code is efficient when you write it as simply and cleanly as possible. For example, using a loop for a command that is repeated many times, or writing procedure for a group of commands are frequently resused are example of writing code efficiently.

execute Run the computer program, or run a smaller section of code such as an individual procedure.

frequency distribution A frequency distribution shows how many of each type or outcome there is in a group. The group is called a sample or a population. You may use variables to show the count (frequency) of each item in the group, for example, shoe sizes among a classroom of students.

global procedure A procedure that can be executed by every element in the project (objects, variables, and other elements if they exist). In MicroWorlds EX, global procedures are written in the Procedures pane.

graphical user interface (GUI) The screen that people see and interact with when using your app. It usually shows buttons, images, objects, menus, text boxes, and other visual elements.

heading Heading is the direction in which an object is pointed. Heading is measured from 0 to 360 degrees, clockwise, with 0 and 360 degrees pointing the object to the top of the workspace.

incrementing Changing a variable value a little bit at a time. Values can be decreased or increased. For example, `bobo,` `setsize size + 2` increases the size of a turtle named bobo by 2.

local procedures A local procedure can only be run by the object that contains it. In MicroWorlds EX, a local procedure is written at the Procedures tab of the backpack of an object.

loop A loop executes a command over and over again, either forever or for a specific number of repetitions.

origin The exact center of the workspace, located at the coordinates (0, 0).

primitive A command that is built into the programming language. For example, home is a primitive in MicroWorlds EX that sends the turtle to the center of the workspace and gives it a heading of 0.

procedure A new command you create and name. A procedure combines primitives and other procedures, in a specific sequence, possibly with branches and loops. Once created, you can use the procedure in your program.

random Randomness is important to make simulations more realistic and games and toys more fun and challenging. In MicroWorlds EX, the command `random 6` can make any of these numbers: 0, 1, 2, 3, 4, 5, or 6. This can be used to simulate a roll of a single die. Additionally, the command `pick` can be used to randomly select objects in a list. For example, `setsh pick [boy girl]` randomly picks either a boy or a girl, where `boy` and `girl` are the names of shapes, and applies it to the active turtle.

shape A shape is worn by a turtle to make it look like something other than a turtle. There are shapes available in the Painting/Clipart palette, and you can make your own original shapes in the Shape Editor. Some programming languages refer to shapes as *costumes*.

simulation A pretend version, or model, of a real event. Simulations can help you understand something faster or easier than watching real world events.

text handling Putting together text in certain ways, usually for display to the user.

text-to-speech Changing printed text into spoken words (audio).

timer The MicroWorlds EX timer counts in tenths of a second. When one second has passed, it shows the number 10. To show the real number of seconds, you have to take the number on the timer and divide by 10: `timer / 10`.

syntax The grammar (where the words go) and punctuation (parentheses, brackets, commas, and quotes) of a programming language.

turtle (object) The name MicroWorlds EX uses for an object. The turtle can wear shapes so that it does not look like a turtle.

universal color conditional A command that runs when any object touches the chosen color. Universal means that any turtle walking across the color (or mouse clicking the color) will cause the instructions to be executed. Universal color conditionals function only on background colors, not turtle colors and not colors in shapes worn by turtles.

variable A quantity that can have different values at different times.

workspace The area where you create the background, objects, and user interface that people will see when they use your app.

DEDICATION

Celebrating Ian and Carson and their earliest ventures in coding.

ABOUT THE AUTHOR

Camille McCue has loved STEM (science, technology, engineering, and mathematics) her entire life. When she was your age, her favorite toys were her Radio Shack 300-in-1 electronics kit, her chemistry set, her Lite-Brite, and her Operation game. Her very first computer was a Timex-Sinclair ZX80, hooked up to a television set that went haywire during weekly vacuuming.

Camille earned her math degree at the University of Texas at Austin. She earned her advanced degrees in curriculum and instruction with her doctoral research at UNLV focused on tween coding. Professionally, Camille has worked for IBM, PBS, and NASA, and has taught STEM courses throughout her career to students just like you. She currently serves as the Director of Technology Innovations for the Adelson Educational Campus in Las Vegas. *Getting Started with Coding* is Camille's seventh technology book.

AUTHOR'S ACKNOWLEDGMENTS

Thanks to the amazing team at Wiley for their hard work in assembling *Getting Started with Coding*. As always, I owe a huge debt of gratitude to Executive Editor Steve Hayes for his incredible vision and support over the years. I am also greatly appreciative of my Development Editor, Brian Walls, and the many hours he and Project Layout Lead, Galen Gruman, invested in bringing this exciting new design to fruition! I also owe an enormous thanks to Barnes & Noble for pursuing this special venture to introduce kids to coding.

I would also like to acknowledge Michael Quinn of Logo Computer Systems Inc. (LCSI), LCSI for making available the fabulous MicroWorlds EX software, as well as Dr. Seymour Papert, the man who long ago envisioned children using computers as tools for expressing creativity through his Logo programming environment.

Most of all, a giant "Thank you!" to my brilliant boys, Ian and Carson, for their valuable insight and input regarding project ideas and execution; and to my sweet and supportive husband, Michael. Many thanks also to my spectacular students throughout the years who have honed my thinking and my teaching — I have enjoyed working with every one of you. And finally, thank you to my parents, Beverly and Eric, who skimped and saved to buy me all those STEM tools that helped me develop into the person I am today.

PUBLISHER'S ACKNOWLEDGMENTS

Executive Editor: Steven Hayes

Development Editor: Brian Walls

Sr. Content Development & Assembly Manager: Mary Corder

Sr. Editorial Assistant: Cherie Case

Special Help: Christine Corry

Project Layout: Galen Gruman

Creative Director: Paul Dinovo

Marketing: Melisa Duffy, Lauren Noens, Raichelle Weller

Launch Consultants: John Helmus, John Scott